Self and Society

DEDICATED TO

LAURANCE S. ROCKEFELLER

WITHOUT WHOM NOT

Self and Society

Studies in the Evolution of Consciousness

William Irwin Thompson

ia

IMPRINT ACADEMIC

Published in the UK by Imprint Academic
PO Box 200, Exeter EX5 5YX, UK

Published in the USA by Imprint Academic
Philosophy Documentation Center
PO Box 7147, Charlottesville, VA 22906-7147, USA

ISBN 0 907845 827

A CIP catalogue record for this book is available from the
British Library and US Library of Congress

Contents

INTRODUCTION

Studies in the Evolution of Culture

The studies in this volume grew out of my eighteen-year collabora-
tion with the chaos mathematician Ralph Abraham, so I would like
to put this work on cultural history into the cultural history of my
own work with my Lindisfarne Association colleagues in the period
of the last two decades of the twentieth century.

In the 1980s, a group of video and electronic artists, computer scientists, mathematicans, and 'new edgey' sorts of thinkers was
founded in Los Angeles by the late Andra Akers and called Synergy
International. In the fall of 1985, I was in New York, conducting a
symposium on the Gaia theory of Lovelock and Margulis[1] when
Andra asked me to come to Los Angeles for the weekend to give an
informal talk at the Los Angeles Film Institute in response to what I
would see there in a conference cum performance of artists in the
new electronic and computing media.[2] As part of this gathering,
Andra arranged a party at her house in West Hollywood in which all
the artists and scientists took part. One of the people I just had to
meet, Andra insisted, was the mathematician and chaos theorist
from the University of California at Santa Cruz, Ralph Abraham.
Since I had recently read some articles about chaos theory in *The Scientific American*, I was quite interested, but also somewhat afraid, for
like many people in the humanities, I suffer from a severe case of
'math anxiety'. Much to my surprise and delight, Ralph was inter-

---

[1]   This colloquium subsequently became the book *Gaia: A Way of Knowing*
(Lindisfarne Press, Great Barrington, MA, 1987).

[2]   International Synergy published the proceedings of this conference, *Is Journal
#1*, 1986, ISSN 0887-946X, and this monograph became the pilot issue of a
journal which carried on for about ten years.

ested in everything — art, religion, science, as well as mathematics — and was not at all interested in controling experience with abstractions. Not at all like so many of the scientific reductionists I had met before, Ralph and his attraction to chaos theory seemed energized precisely because of an interest in the relationship between lively intellectual structures and living forms in nature. Looking more like a countercultural Jerry Garcia than an Olympian Albert Einstein, Ralph was not intimidating, so I began to open up to his way of thinking, one that seemed to fit in well with the complex planetary dynamics of the Gaia theory, and one also that seemed to offer a way out of the rigidity of 'sacred geometry' that in our Lindisfarne Summer School on Sacred Architecture under Keith Critchlow's charismatic mastery had fast become an authoritarian platonic cult. I was looking for a way out of the closed, esoteric, and rigid geometry of containment in an unchanging eternity, and there in Ralph's chaos theory, a door to another way of understanding the geometry of the phase portraits of complex systems seemed to open up.

At the time I had met Ralph, I had just published my science fiction novel, *Islands Out of Time*,[3] which expressed my allergic rejection of the organ transplant of European anti-democratic platonism to the Lindisfarne Summer Institute in Crestone, Colorado, but I was also at work on a shift from cultural history to cultural ecology.

The founder of the United Nations' Environmental Program Maurice Strong had organized a conference in New York in February of 1983 in which he asked various environmental activists and thinkers from around the world to take part. Strong had organized the Stockholm Conference in 1972, and this had been responsible for the establishment of the United Nations new program on the environment; now Strong was continuing with the work that would lead to the Rio Summit on the Global Ecology in 1992. Strong had also donated the land for the establishment of Lindisfarne in Crestone, Colorado and had taken part in one of our Lindisfarne Fellows conferences on ecology, in which the Fellows and a group of about eighty people took part. Among them were Amory and Hunter Lovins, John and Nancy Todd, David Orr, Hazel Henderson, Wendell Berry, David Ehrenfeld, Wes and Dana Jackson, James Lovelock, Sim Van der Ryn, Paolo Soleri, and Gary Snyder. The Lin-

---

[3]   *Islands Out of Time: A Memoir of the Last Days of Atlantis* (Dial Press: New York, 1985).

disfarne Fellows presented an understanding of ecology and governance that was in advance of the Leftist position that Strong enjoyed in the world of national governments, NGOs, and multinational corporations. The UN conference he organized at the Waldorf Astoria in New York was a reflection on the global predicament seen ten years after Stockholm and ten years before the Rio Conference to come. In recognition of the Lindisfarne approach, I was invited to come to give a talk and to take part in a swanky black tie dinner for the global notables. I declined the invitation to the black tie dinner, as black ties and tuxedos give me cultural contact dermatitis, but I did agree to give a brief talk in which I offered another way of looking at Western Civilization as a movement through 'Four Cultural Ecologies'.

The satellite perspective of history that I offered was so lofty that the talk had as much impact on the audience as a passing cloud, and I remember being followed by a more conventional presentation by David Lilienthal, a founding father of the Atomic Energy Commission, and he spoke of the need for more economic growth and the construction of more nuclear reactors. I retreated to my customary solitude in Bern, Switzerland, and the talk was subsequently published in the Green activist journal *Resurgence* [4] — which is certainly a case of 'preaching to the choir'.

In spite of the lack of interest in this new approach, I was quite taken with the shift from intellectual history to cultural ecology and continued to work on expanding the brief talk into a more fully developed essay. I was in the middle of this work in Bern when I received Ralph's paper, 'Mathematics and Evolution', which he sent me as a follow-up to our meeting in Los Angeles. The essay was very brief — a kind of intellectual telegram, which is often Ralph's favoured mode of expression — and was just about as fast and schematic as my talk in New York had been; but it had enormous impact on me, for suddenly I saw that the four cultural-ecologies that I was describing had not only four associated literary forms of narrative but four greater mentalities in which mathematical exposition and literary narrative were inseparably united in a historical world-view. Everything fell into place in one of those 'Eureka' kinds of peak experiences that give the intellectual life its unique joy. I rewrote my essay, working in this new theory of literary-mathematical mentalities that are embedded in cultural ecolo-

---

[4]   See *Resurgence*, November-December, 1983, No. 101, 16-17.

gies, and sent off the revised version just in time for it to make it into my new book, *Pacific Shift*, as the chapter entitled 'The Four Cultural-Ecologies of the West'.

Intellectual peak experiences are, I guess, by their nature rather isolated and isolating ones, for this book, much like the talk I gave in New York, had absolutely no impact and it went out of print within a year or two of its publication and never made it into paperback, except for two small and very obscure editions in German and Japanese. But Ralph and I carried on with our dialogue and I arranged a meeting of the Lindisfarne Fellows at Esalen in Big Sur, California in which Mary Catherine Bateson, James Lovelock and Francisco Varela interacted with Ralph. As these interactions continued to develop, they became expressed in my next book, *Imaginary Landscape: Making Worlds of Myth and Science*.

Our next collaborative project was to be an effort to unite mathematics and art in a performance at the high altar of the Cathedral of St. John the Divine in New York of what I called Electronic Stained Glass. Through the use of an enormous screen, a video projector, a superfast computer, and performances by three mathematicians using a modified stringed instrument and two piano keyboards, invisible micro-structures of time were presented as visual geometries of the phase-portrait of their behavior in our world of slower, human time. As part of the evening's presentation, I did one riff with the band in which I read a poem combined with footage of spirochetes taken from the microscope filmings at Lynn Margulis's lab that I had edited and made into a music video, and that Ralph then set to theme and computerized variation. With an audience of about 300 people, we presented our scientifically avant garde experiment in the vault of that enormous Gothic cathedral. This performance of 'MIMI and the Illuminati' was intended to be more a moment of *Wissenskunst* than *Wissenschaft*. It was enormous fun and though certainly too experimental to be yet great art — more like a child's kaleidoscope than a rose window from Chartres — it was, nevertheless, an event unlike anything any of those present had seen before.

This expression of a form of presentation that was not simply mathematics and not simply art set Ralph and me to thinking about the whole relationship between mathematics and art, and in conversations at the Cathedral with the architect Santiago Calatrava, and other Lindisfarne Fellows — the atmospheric chemist James Lovelock, the biologist John Todd, and the botanists Paul and Julie Mankiewicz — we worked on the design of a bioshelter for the roof of the Cathedral in which Lovelock would design electron capture devices that would read the atmosphere interacting with the exhalations of the visitors and Ralph would create the Visual Math software and hardware to transform that gaseous interaction into an interactive video art form in a more permanent installation of 'electronic stained glass'. Some of the videos were to be mimetic, some interactive, and some composed in advance by musicians and video artists. But the project was never to be, for the 'Green Dean' of the Cathedral, the Very Reverend James Morton, was blocked and then retired by the very prosaic Episcopal Bishop Grein. He objected to having trees and a bioshelter set on high in a cathedral, and so he worked hard to replace Dean Morton with a new Dean, one who was more conventionally Episcopal and less imaginatively ecological. The project was too utopian and its costs far too celestial for a city suffering from the more immediate crises of AIDS and crack. But practicality has its costs as well and the Cathedral of St. John the Divine has now become a very large, empty, and stone-cold space.

We all went our separate ways, and my way took me to San Francisco to give a series of lectures on 'literature and the evolution of consciousness' at the California Institute of Integral Studies. The journey gave me more opportunities to go down to Santa Cruz to work with Ralph, and in presentations we gave at C.I.I.S. and Esalen, we continued to try to take the project a few steps further. As part of the work in preparing my lectures, I brought along a small figurine, a copy of the paleolithic statuette of Lespugue, that I had bought at the museum shop in the Louvre in Paris. As I studied the statue, it seemed to me that the head was a unit of measure, and that the most unrealistic rendering of the body seemed to divide up into sections that I thought possibly could express some canon of proportion — something like, length of head is to chest as chest is to thighs: a prehistoric version of the classical canon of Praxeteles. I suggested to Ralph that he scan the figure and then study it mathematically to see if there was anything interesting going on in the figure as icon. Ralph found the little statue to express a visual correlate to the heptatonic scale and his mathematical confirmation of my artistic hunch makes up the material of the first chapter of his new book, *Bolts from the Blue: Mathematics and Cultural Evolution*.

As Ralph and I continued to carry on our discussion by e-mail, from Zurich to Santa Cruz, concerning works of art and the progression of the historical mentalities — the Arithmetic, Geometric, Galilean Dynamical, and Chaotic — Ralph cautioned me and said, 'But what about the algebraic?' I asked him what he saw as the essence of the algebraic mentality and he responded with a note about the entrancement with the purity of a transcendental notation. I asked for more time to think about it.

The next morning I e-mailed back to Ralph that the entrancement with code, with a substitution of the mental for the material, seemed to express itself at the time of the emergence of algebra in the art of calligraphy circa 800, in the beautiful Arabic Korans and Celtic Gospels. Indeed, the genius of Islam itself is expressed in the sublimation of concrete idols in favour of an invisible Allah registered on Earth by an angelic intermediary in a transcendental script. Coeval with the emergence of algebra was alchemy, and, in its Alexandrian origins, it was concerned with the subliming of base lead into ethereal gold, script into scripture. Certainly, medieval allegory expressed a mentality completely fascinated with the emblematic power of an esoteric code.

But the more I thought about the algebraic mentality, the more I thought that it had never really become as globally extensive as the geometrical, which externalized itself in the expressions of architecture all around the world, from Mesopotamia to Egypt, India, China, Mesoamerica, and medieval Europe. The geometer of the kind of civilization that expressed itself in classical and high medieval architecture was not simply a technician but more like a public health officer responsible for the harmony and just proportion of the polity; he was more of a Pythagoras or Confucius than a wild Gallois or a paranoid Gödel.

The thought of paranoid Gödel, who starved himself to death because he was afraid that people were trying to poison him, made me stop to reflect on the paranoid's fascination with secret code, with an entrancement for notation that held the sacred hieroglyphs of cosmic meaning. The substitution of code for concrete experience is a primary characteristic of the 'paranoid cosmic synthesis' in which everything is explained. I thought of all the paranoid conspiracy mail that I had received over the years: manuscripts without any margin, with a whole separate text circling around the central transcription, and with keywords like 'world order' or 'Rothschilds and Rockefellers' colored over with highlighting pens. The paranoid had a terror of empty spaces; no space could be left unfilled or uncolonized by his imperious obsession.

When I was living in Bern, I became acquainted with the psychotic art of Adolf Wölfli, for the Kunstmuseum in Bern holds his primary collection. Wölfli is so great an artist that it seems unfair to pigeon-hole him in the category of psychotic art. Psychosis may have driven Wölfli and given him his 'horror vacui' and provided the content for his visions, but his uses of multiple spaces, his sense of design and structure, raise him to the level of art as art and not just psychotic art and clinical data. In Wölfli's 1904 work he was coeval with Cubism in breaking down linear perspective, and in his 'Samoaaden Brücke' he envisions the bridge from multiple and simultaneous perspectives. Rational, linear perspective is abandoned and space becomes curved as beings from multiple dimensions leak through the holes in space and time. Thinking of Ralph's comments about the 'entrancement with notation', I went back to give Wölfli another look, and much to my astonishment I found that Wölfli had written an 'Ode to Algebra', that he had filled in whole notebooks to algebra with his fascinations with cosmic calligraphy and esoteric notation.[5] Perhaps, I thought, Wölfli was the end of a process, the algebraic mentality carried to its extreme.

The coeval emergence of calligraphy and algebra represented a bifurcation, a fork in the road in which one line moved into entrancement with notation and the replacement of the concrete with code in a very introverted form of cosmic solitude, while the other line of descent moved in a more extroverted manner toward the Galilean Dynamical mentality with its movements of global capital and ballistic artillery that transformed the world in what became the shift from medievalism to modernism.[6] One path led into the solitude of cabbalistic magisters who thought that they alone under-

[5]   Adolf Wölfli: Schreiber, Dichter, Zeichner, Componist (Herausgegeben von der Adolf-Wölfli Stiftung Kunstmuseum Bern, Wiese Verlag, Basel, 1997). The Ode to Algebra is on p. 131.

[6]   Alfred W. Crosby sees this shift as occuring before the Renaissance. 'Then, between 1250 and 1350, there came, not so much in theory as in actual application, a marked shift. We can probably pare that century down to fifty years, 1275 to 1325'. See his *The Measure of Reality: Quantification and and Western Society 1250-1600* (Cambridge University Press: Cambridge and New York, 1997), p. 18. Since this is the time of Giotto and Dante, it makes some sense as to see the intellectual breakthrough occurring then, followed by the calamity of the Black Death, and then the economic and social reconstruction of Europe that we associate with Florentine capitalism and Renaissance art. Cultural historians as different as Alfred Crosby and Rudolf Steiner both see the thirteenth century as the time of the bifurcation in the evolution of consciousness, so perhaps it is more informed to push the Renaissance back, before the Black Death. The new mentality would then be seen to be expressed in Arabic music and poetry, inspiring Provencal poetry and Dante's *dulce stil nuovo*, as well as the new

stood the world, and the other to the military-industrial complex of those who sought to rule the world and not simply understand it in some esoteric notation. And not until the cabbalistic notation of a small band of mathematical physicists transformed the outer world with the atom bomb did these roads reconverge. Now in the new mathematical mentality of chaos dynamics, it would seem as if all the historical mentalities are being synthesized in algebraic formulae in which the phase portraits of the geometry of behavior of complex dynamical systems are creating a new evolutionary niche for Artificial Life in which mathematical entities and mathematical domains have their own ontological uprising. Like the holes in space in which other ontological domains leak into ours in the paintings of Adolf Wölfli, other realities, Virtual, Virtuous, and perhaps Unvirtuous as well, are leaking into our conventional world.

Ralph Abraham and I have come to our contemporary cultural bifurcation from two different lines of cultural descent that touched us when we were young assistant professors at Princeton and MIT in the sixties, but we do imagine together that the art and science of this new emergent culture is not going to be an embodiment of the reductionism and eliminativism of the present, or the past five hundred years. Neither abstract nor concrete, this new way of knowing seems to us to be a kind of visual math that is also musical, and perhaps just that kind of music of Strings the Calabi-Yau topologies make as they pulse with the fabric of space-time in ways imaginable for heads that have the heart for it.[7] To get ready for this new planetary culture, we climb and turn on the spiral and blink our eyes in wonder and disbelief as we see a history we missed in the settled cities of the plain where the universities lie.

---

mathematical sensibility. The Algebraic mentality could then be seen as a transition state between the Geometrical and the Gailean Dynamical to come.

[7]   See Brian Greene, *The Elegant Universe: Superstrings, Hidden Dimensions, and the Quest for the Ultimate theory* (New York: W. W. Norton, 1999), pp. 207, 208.

CHAPTER 1

The Evolution of the Afterlife

Even for those who do not believe in a life after death, the idea of the afterlife that a past culture held can serve as a marker in the evolution of human consciousness. Like a demarcation that begins a process of map-making, the description of the time and space of the life after death starts a process of exploring the nature of consciousness and the cultural ideas of individuation that derive from it. World literature is the chronicle of this cultural process of individuation, and literary works of the past serve as milestones on the historical path of the moral and psychological development of humanity.

Our earliest literary mapping of the boundary between the realms of the living and the dead is expressed in ancient Sumerian literature as the journey by the living to the underworld of death, specifically in 'Inanna's Descent into the Netherworld' and Enkidu's descent in the poems of the Gilgamesh cycle.[1] Inanna is a goddess, and her descent into the underworld is a cosmological function, the passage of the evening star under the horizon to arise after its journey through darkness in the underworld as the morning star, but Enkidu in the Gilgamesh cycle is a mortal, and his experience of the journey into the realm of the dead is no triumphant reconstitution of cosmic order but a very sad confrontation with a realm of physical and emotional appetites that are frustrated by the lack of a body with which to satisfy them.

> . . . the house where none leave who have entered it . . . Where dust is their fare and clay their food. (Wolkstein and Kramer, 1983, p.159)

---

[1] For detailed discussions of this literature, see Thompson (1981; 1998).

This sublunary world is the enclosure for mortals. For the Old Kingdom Egyptians during the period of the construction of the Great Pyramids, a god or a god-like Pharoah might think of transcending the world of the physical body and its associated subtle body of life-energy, the *ka*, to return in his star body, or *Sahu*, to his native star in the belt of Orion, but commoners and heroes were doomed to remain in the form of their shade, their *ba*, restricted to the sublunary world.[2] Even the ghost of the great hero Achilles laments his existence as a shade, as he cries out to the living Odysseus who does not, like the Sumerian Enkidu, actually descend into the underworld but merely stands at the sacrificial pit that serves as the threshold between the worlds of the living and the dead:

> 'We ranked you with immortals in your lifetime,
> We Argives did, and here your power is royal
> Among the dead men's shades. Think, then,
> Akhilleus: You need not be so pained by death.'
> To this He answered swiftly:
> 'Let me hear no smooth talk
> of death from you, Odysseus, light of councils.
> Better, I say, to break sod as a farm hand
> for some poor country man, on iron rations,
> than lord it over all the exhausted dead.'

(*Odyssey*, Book XI, ll. 571–81, p. 201).

As a product of culture, human existence is collective in its very nature, and just as it was collective in life, so is it in death. A king or a hero may reign among his servants in a shadowy copy of his former personality, or a tribal man may rest among his ancestors, but enlightenment and personal transcendence of the world of appetites and passions in the shame-culture of the tribe is beyond imagining. The soul of man is still caught in the evolutionary residue of a folk soul, or animal group soul, and the best one's shade can hope for is to gain a momentary florescence in the act of being remembered by one's group or descendants — and this is still the case today in Mexico with the archaic rituals of *el dia de los muertos*.

The Axial Age, with its global epiphany of prophets, from Orpheus and Pythagoras to Isaiah II, Buddha, Lao Tzu and

---

[2]   The Middle Kingdom experienced a democratization with the expanding population. 'The Coffin Texts eliminated the royal exclusivity of the Pyramid Texts, putting the texts at the disposal of all deceased persons and thus making the enjoyment of the afterlife something that all could attain; now, every deceased person was an Osiris NN' (Hornung, 1999, p. 9).

Quetzalcoatl, seems to mark a critical turning point in the evolution of consciousness, for now the individual soul seems capable of knowing and expressing a higher truth than the received wisdom of the ancestors, the idols of the tribe. Eric Havelock has described this transition as the evolution from the life-force of the Homeric *thymos* to the Socratic *psyche*:

> At some time toward the end of the fifth century before Christ, it became possible for a few Greeks to talk about their 'souls' as though they had selves or personalities which were autonomous and not fragments of the atmosphere nor of a cosmic life force, but what we might call entities or real substances (Havelock, 1991, p. 197).

Orphism was the vehicle in which this transition from *thymos* to *psyche* became articulated in hymns and instructions to the living on how to make their passage in the realm of the dead.

Orphism was a religion with a belief in immortality and in posthumous rewards and punishments. So far so good. But it had a more individual doctrine than that. Hades, with its prospect of torment and feasting, was not the end. There was the doctrine of the circle of birth, or cycle of births, and the possibility of ultimate escape from reincarnation to the state of perfected divinity (Guthrie, 1993, p. 164).

The figure of Orpheus, like that of Pythagoras or Quetzalcoatl, is a being of legend, so his story is more myth than history and serves as an allegorical performance of the truths to be passed from an initiate in the mysteries to the aspiring novice. Like Quetzalcoatl in Mesoamerica, he is a reformer who seeks to eliminate human sacrifice and carry humanity forward in its evolution from sorcery and blood magic to myth and a more stellar spirituality.[3]

Just as Enkidu was warned not to partake of the food of the dead, less he be trapped in their underworld, so Orpheus is warned not to look back as he seeks to bring his beloved into light. In the esoteric

---

[3] For translations and an introductory essay, see Thompson (1983). For a different interpretation, see Florescano (1999); see p. 135 for his discussion of Olmec ceremonial centres. For the presence of the iconography of the Plumed Serpent in Olmec culture, see Gurthrie (1996), p. 84. My own poetic and speculative interpretation is that the poetry and the artifacts show a conflict between an archaic shamanic tradition and an emergent prophetic religion. In the archaic tradition of animal possession, the shaman projects his subtle body into a jaguar and brings about the birth of a half-human, half-jaguar baby. To propitiate this spirit, human sacrifice of foetuses in the womb are offered up — hence the presence of all these infants with jaguar features. Quetzalcoatl tries to suppress this tradition with a higher morality, and he establishes his palace and temple, but the sorcerers come to bring him down and return to their archaic ways of human sacrifice.

practice of yoga nidra — the yoga of sleep meditation — the realm of imagery is an intermediate world of perception and deception, and only the realm of the *nadam*, of the cosmic sound, can enable the practioner of yoga to reappropriate the realm of deep dreamless sleep in the waking state of clear mind — a state of consciousness called *samadhi*.

Orpheus, as a musician of the heavenly harp given to him by Apollo, is an initiate of this cosmic sound — this music of the heavenly spheres — but according to the mysteries, our human star nature has been mixed with the ashes of the Titans at our emergence on Earth, and so humanity is a dyadic and contradictory creature. Our spirit is split between body and soul, between Orpheus and Euridyce. Because our star spirit has been captured in the vestiges of the elemental spirits of earth and matter, we must rescue it by shifting consciousness away from the concrete density of visual imagery to the higher realm of imageless music. But Orpheus looks back, seeking to hold his soul in sight, and so he loses her entirely. As he returns to earth, alone and embittered, he spurns the love of women and becomes a lover of men. The metaphoric complementarity of male and female as a trope for the polarity of the incarnate being is lost.

This mythic trope, as allegory for initiates, is describing a blocking of the union of ego and psyche, or waking mind and dreaming mind, in a psychological implosion of the ego in narcissism: same is bonding to same in a projected form of self love. But the male body, beautiful or not, can never serve as an answer to the problem of death. Just as the Goddess Ishtar sought her revenge against the male-bonding and defiance of the heroes Gilgamesh and Enkidu, so now the Maeneads seek their revenge against the violation of archaic women's mysteries. The blood sacrifice that the reformer Orpheus had sought to eliminate is inflicted on him as he is torn to pieces by the Maeneads — those vestiges of the neolithic matristic culture of the sacrificial dying male and the enduring Great Mother.

In the terms of Jean Gebser's schema for the evolution of consciousness, Orpheus is the figure that marks the transition from the Magical to the Mythic structure of consciousness.[4] But the collective wins out, and just as the Renaissance was followed by the Inquisition and a new baroque economy of slavery with its extravagant dis-

---

[4]   Gebser's is one of an unfoldment of structures of consciousness through Archaic, Magical, Mythical, Mental and Integral. See Gebser (1984).

play of wealth, so Orpheus's Apollonian reforms are followed by sacrificial rituals and his story is reappropriated into a cultural narrative of Dionysian ecstasy. The *psyche* remains trapped in the intermediate realm of imagery and the mind's identification of consciousness with imagery — the familiar world in which 'seeing is believing'.

But human spiritual evolution is not entirely stopped, and the reforms of the Axial Age are partially absorbed as Greek culture carries on with its transition from the Homeric *thymos* to the Orphic *psyche* — from the Bardic oral culture of the Archaic era to the new literate culture of the sacred text of the Classical era. As Steve Farmer has argued, it is the very portability of the new writing materials that serves to construct the Axial Age and spread the new values from India to Greece with Pythagoreanism in one direction, and from India to China with Buddhism in the other direction of the Silk Road.[5] Indeed, in the evolution of consciousness from oral culture to literate civilization, the sacred text itself becomes the oxymoron that embodies our contradictory human nature. The text exists in the realm of imagery and is visually read, but it calls us back to a recollection (anamnesis) of our stellar nature. Death itself becomes less biological and collective — as it was in the neolithic and megalithic eras of collective burials — and becomes in the Classical era, more *psycho*logical and personal.

The shift from aural to alphabetic consciousness, as articulated by cultural historians like Marshall McLuhan, Eric Havelock and more recently Leonard Shlain (1998), is an external, sociological way of perceiving this cultural transformation. Steve Farmer's argument that the portability of writing materials served to stimulate the efflorescence of archaistic syncretisms in the face of innovation is another way of expressing McLuhan's tetrad that one new medium obsolesces a current medium and retrieves a previously obsolesced medium. In my own work and in Paolo Soleri's work in the 1970s — through the influence of Teilhard de Chardin's concepts — we termed this process 'miniaturization'.[6]

---

[5]   Lecture given at the Ross Institute, New York, August, 2001. See Farmer (1998), p. 96.

[6]   'What will enable the metaindustrial village to become more than a stagnant pond is the interiorization of consciousness, through new forms of contemplative education, and the miniaturization of technology' (Thompson, 1978, p. 93).

The inheritor of the contributions of the Axial Age of Pythagoras and Orpheus is, of course, Plato. But Plato does not put his faith in music as the yoga for uniting body and spirit; his distrust of the world of the senses leads him to reject the passionate stirrings of modal music and for his perfect utopian society, he send the poets into exile. In the place of Orphic music and poetry, he celebrates the abstract and the sublimed geometrical, fleshless figure in the new genre of philosophy. Plato's myths are not the kind that they were for Orpheus; they are mythic allegories as the new mental code of the soul — 'likely stories' that bridge the divide separating the Sensible and Intelligible worlds. The text that embodies this transition from the Gebserian Mythic to the Mental level of consciousness is the 'Myth of Er' from Plato's *Republic*.

In this 'likely story' with which he ends this dialogue, Plato shifts from the dialectical search for the nature of truth, to the dramatic mode of myth and story. In a way, the dialogue has prepared us for this shift, for it opens with a description of the Panathenaic procession in which horseman passes the torch to horseman, and this serves as a trope for the rational soul seated atop the beast of the physical body and passing the torch of the search for truth from speaker to speaker as the dialogue progresses. But logic and the dialectical method only take us so far. Ultimately the Orphic and Pythagorean Plato returns to myth and ends his dialectical inquiry into the nature of justice with a tale of karma, forgetfulness and souls falling like shooting stars to their next birth, and their next chance to redeem themselves in a process of metempsychosis and moral refinement of their coarse appetites and passions. This essential text marks more than the first imagining of a political utopia, it expresses in itself the evolutionary shift from the shame-culture of the tribe to the guilt-culture of the individual (see Dodd, 1951), for the afterlife Er describes is now presented in moral and karmic terms of reward and punishment for one's individual actions in life. Escape from the collective in individual transcendence and enlightenment can now be envisioned for any man, and not just a Pharoah, a Pythagorean initiate or the yogic hermit of the Upanishads.

A more physiological and internal way of considering this cultural transformation from the Homeric *thymos* to the Orphic *psyche* was articulated in the seventies by the psychologist Julian Jaynes in his book *The Origin of Consciousness in the Breakdown of the Bicameral*

Mind (1976).[7] Indeed, one can argue that the whole movement of Consciousness Studies that followed was greatly advanced by this seminal work. Jaynes argued that Achilles' somnambulistic consciousness came from the projection of the processing of the imagistic mode of the right hemisphere into external space. Visions were experienced as literally taking place, so in the 'Anger of Achilles' Athena could be seen and felt by Achilles to restrain his anger and sword, though no one else saw Athena. Jaynes further argued that the corpus callosum was not yet functionally orchestrated to integrate the activities of the hemispheres and to recategorize hypnagoic activities exclusively to the dream-state.

Jaynes drew heavily on the German Classicist Bruno Snell's book, *The Discovery of the Mind* (1982). But like many Classical scholars, Snell was not familiar with contemplative practices or even with Egyptian ideas concerning the subtle bodies, so Snell did not recognize that the Homeric *thymos* was not a Greek invention but simply a Greek translation of the Egyptian *ka*. In his understandable enthusiasm for his own fascinating insights and discoveries, Jaynes let go of the reins of scholarly restraint and tried to alter the chronology of literary texts to fit his theory. So the *Gilgamesh Epic* — which seemed too psychologically advanced to be so early — had to be redated and made to take on the date of its last copy in the Library of Ashurbanipal. Thus for Jaynes, the cultural transformation of the Axial Age was not caused by the rise of alphabetic and ideographic technologies or their transcultural portability; these were outward expressions of an evolutionary mutation in cerebral organization. It would not be until the 1980s and '90s that the new sciences of complexity, as popularized by the Chaos Collective at the University of California at Santa Cruz and the Santa Fe Institute, would help people to see that causation is rarely singular and linear, and that most often an emergent domain is brought forth through bottom-up chains of mutiple and mutually interacting agents. Gebser, McLuhan, Havelock, Jaynes, Steve Farmer and I were all seeing aspects of the cultural phenomenology of the evolution of consciousness, but were focusing on what was closest to our own immediate world of experience.

---

[7] In my own lectures from this time, I was more critical of Jaynes — because of his Procrustean bed approach — than I would be now. Now I am more appreciative of his contribution in stimulating the growth of the new field of consciousness studies. See Thompson (1981/1996).

Nothing is clearer when one goes from the epic of the *Iliad* to the *Odyssey* than that something has happened in the world view of humanity. Indeed, one of the reasons that I accepted the old eighteenth-century idea of 'Die Homerishe Frage' — in which there are two Homers and not one — is because the *Odyssey* is so different in world view from the *Iliad*. Crafty Odysseus does not have the archaic somnambulistic consciousness of Achilles; his mind is clear, corpuscular and discreet; he stands at the threshold of the underworld, but does not cross over or descend. Aeneas, the demigod as son of Venus, is able to descend, into the underworld, but even he must be accompanied by the archaic figure of the Cumaen sybil. Yet even in the case of the shamanistic sybil, human consciousness is now so discreet and stabile — and no longer fluid and astrally permeable — that the god has to break in upon her if she is to become conscious of the visionary realms and prophesy. The image that Virgil presents is of the god breaking in a wild stallion. In the simile of a horseman forcing a bridle into the mouth of a wild horse, the god is presented as a hostile mode of consciousness that must be thrust into the mind and mouth of the sybil if he is to control her and speak prophetically out of her body.[8]

It is this ancient Greek vision of the Elysian Field of Plato's Myth of Er that Virgil both inherits and recalls, and it is clear in the entire narrative of the *Aeneid* that the kairos of Virgil in its cultural process of individuation has passed from the *thymos* of Homer to the *psyche* of Plato and on to the worldly ego with its dutiful sense of self in the illustrious example of '*pius Aeneas*'. In fact, the architectonic structure of the *Aeneid*, with its movement from Western Asia to Western Europe, and its soldierly rejection of love for a female Queen in favour of the founding of a patriarchal empire, is a recapitulation of an earlier movement from matristic to patriarchal, and is a newly energized performance of the shift from collectivist Asia to individualistic Rome with its grand imperial theatre of personal ambition, of arms and the man. But implicit in this shift from East to West is also an archetypal shift from psyche to ego. It is not the love of woman, or the experiences of the soul in subtle and immaterial realms that are to matter now; it is duty and action in the world; it is the world of Empire. Ego and Empire are co-dependantly originat-

---

[8]   See Aeneid, Book VI, ll. 75–80: 'tanto magis ille fatigat/ os rabidum, fera corda domans, fingitque premendo'.

ing psychological structures, in which humanity now leans more heavily towards rationality than towards psyche.

In terms of cultural evolution, for which mythological and literary texts serve as fossil records, we see here a developmental movement through three stages, or structures, *thymos, psyche* and *ego*. With *thymos*, the focus of attention is on the subtle energy body, the Egyptian ka, or the *pranayamakosha* in yogic psychology (see Mookerjee, 1982, p. 12). In this cultural complex, death seems to be collective, as if humans were still closely identified with the structure of a group soul rather than an individual one. With this formation in archaic Greece and ancient Egypt, we seem to be looking back towards an even more ancient formation of shamanism and animal possession. In Ice-Age art, the shaman is pictured in cave paintings and carvings as a human in animal form, or half-human, half-animal. Religion often preserves an ancient structure and envaluates it to see new formations or levels of cultural organization as evil. In the ancient culture of animal possession and blood sacrifice, Orpheus and Quetzalcoatl are threats to the ways of sorcery and magic. They represent a movement away from possession and group consciousness towards individuation.

At the psychic level of organization, the individual is represented as a dyadic being, one split between conscious and unconscious, between a social life of norms and duty, and a pull backward to the unconscious through erotic transfiguration and death. This dyadic mode of being is polarized between sex and death, so the archetypal iconography for this cultural construction is that of the male body as the waking consciousness and the female soul as the dreaming and visionary consciousness: Orpheus and Euridyce. But as the process of individuation continues to develop in the classical Roman world, there is a reversal of this signification of the soul as feminine and the ego as masculine. In the myth of 'Psyche and Eros', as retold in Apulieus' *Golden Ass*, it is the god who comes by night that is presented as masculine and the receptive personality that is presented as feminine. Indeed, the whole story of the invisible lover who must not be seen seems to echo with mystical allusions that take us back to Gnostic and Kabbalistic sources. The sisters of Psyche, who are jealous of her intimacy with the god, recall the angels who were jealous at the creation of man and refused to bow down and adore God's latest creation — as is told in both the Hebraic Midrash and the Koran. Since the angels and jinn were made of light and fire, they were repelled at adoring a creature made out of mud. If the sisters are thus

an echo of the jealous angels, then Psyche is a trope for the unique-
ness of the human soul and Eros is a metaphor for the indwelling
god, the hidden god that is intimately embedded with its beloved
individual being. The stricture that Psyche is not to try to 'see' the
god is, of course, an echo of the interdiction to Orpheus that he
should not try to turn and 'see' Euridyce as he leads her out of the
underworld. The mystical significance of this trope is that the divine
substratum of the human being is not experienced in the waking or
dreaming consciousness, but only in the fullness of a non-perceptual
mind that is experienced in deep, dreamless sleep. It is this state of
mind that the yogi of the *Upanishads* is taught to try to reappropriate
in the *samadhi* of meditation — a mode of higher consciousness that
is not dreaming or restricted to the perceptual field of wakeful consciousness. What 'Psyche and Eros' represents is an evolution of
consciousness in which a higher self is only available to Mind — as
opposed to conscious awareness — through the higher dimensional
modes beyond three-dimensional perception.

In this evolution of Graeco-Roman culture from psyche to ego,
there arises in the exoteric, secular realm of life a turning away from
the female to the call of duties in the imperial world, and this is
archetypally expressed in Aeneas turning away from Dido to found
Rome and the beginnings of Western Europe. But coeval with this
emergence of egohood in the classical world is a new mythic narrative in which the soul does not simply descend into the underworld,
but journeys upwards through the solar and starlit heavens — as we
see in the Jewish apocalyptic texts of *The Book of Enoch* and the Christian apocryphal *Vision of Paul* (see Barnstone, 1984, pp. 485, 537).
Here the focus of consciousness seems to be shifting from the waking mind to another mode, one that is not unconscious or dreaming
but rather of 'spirit' or a higher mind in which the world is no longer
three dimensional, but has higher dimensionality. If we apply the
yogic terminology of the energy sheaths that constitute the fully
incarnate being, then the *thymos* is the Egyptian *ka*, or the Vedic
pranamayakosa, and the *psyche* is the Egyptian *ba* or the Vedic
manomayakosa, and the journey through the heavens is effected with
the higher minds of the Pharaohonic *Sahu*, or the Vedic
vijnanamayakosa and the *anatamayakosa*.

In ancient Egypt, Osiris became Lord of the Dead, but in the
Judeo-Christian kairos, Christ is presented as more than the Lord of
the shadowy realm of the dead; he is presented as the solar logos, the
risen Lord of all the worlds. The text that marks this transition is the

Gospel of Nicodemus that presents 'Christ's Harrowing of Hell' (Barnstone, 1984, p. 374) and his release of Adam and Eve. Humanity is no longer bound to the sublunary world of life and death, the waking mind and the dreaming mind.

For this developing Christian tradition, it is important to emphasize that 'spiritual' experiences are not taking place in the psychic realm, or out-of-the-body astral travel. These modes of religious practice become devalued and placed down in the realm of sorcery and witchcraft. It is the witch who travels by night to out-of-the-body congresses with shades and demons. So it is important to the author of the third-century apocryphal text, 'The Vision of Paul', to emphasize that his vision of the higher worlds did not transpire while he was dreaming or was in some astral out-of-the body state: 'While I was in the body in which I was snatched up to the third heaven, the word of the Lord came to me . . .' (Jones, 1950, p. 4). In the Islamic continuation of this Judeo-Christian tradition, this journey to the heavens becomes Mohammed's Night Journey — the *Miraj Nama* — and on the basis of this text, Avicenna develops a complex psychology of multiple states of perception and consciousness (see Heath, 1992, pp. 107–44). New directions in Islamic studies are beginning to show how deeply embedded Mohammed's vision is in this Judeo-Christian tradition, and that parts of the Koran in fact derived from pre-existing Christian and Aramaic texts; so, perhaps, world peace may be advanced if we come to appreciate the continuities more than the discontinuities within the Abrahamic religions.[9]

The consummation and, indeed, finishing of this journey through heaven and hell so intensely articulated in the Judeo-Christian and Islamic traditions comes, of course, with Dante's *Divine Comedy*. That Dante was familiar with popular Islamic renderings of Mohammed's Night Journey is now harder to deny than it was when Christians came to the defence of Christianity's supreme genius to reject Asin Palacio's contentions concerning Arabic influences (see Anderson, 1983, p. 277), but even granting these Islamic influences, it is important to recognize that Dante takes the journey to a whole new level of topological complexity. The three realms of hell, purgatory and heaven can be recognized as presenting the medieval architecture of consciousness of vegetative, sensitive and rational functions with their indwelling spirits — as opposed to the Vedic

---

[9]　See Alexander Stille's comments on the scholarship of Christoph Luxenberg in Germany in Stille (2002).

sheaths or *kosas* — that derives from Aristotle's *De Anima* (see Anderson, 1983, p. 109); but in presenting the nature of consciousness in heaven, Dante goes beyond even Aristotle and his Arab commentators in an intuitive and inspired vision of the higher dimensionality of a hypersphere. It was the physicist Mark Peterson who first pointed out that the geometry described in the vision of the primum mobile and the Angel sphere of Canto 28 of the *Paradiso* is that of a 3-sphere (Peterson, 1979).

Contemporary psychology recognizes conscious and unconscious realms, for the brain can respond to stimuli without bothering to go through the realm of the restricted field of conscious awareness. Electroencephalographs of sleeping infants, for example, have shown that an infant's brain is listening and responding to and learning the phonological distinctions of the mother's language even while it is sleeping (see Cheour *et al.*, 2002). Lullabies, therefore, are not a frivolous exercise for mother and infant! So the conscious/unconscious distinction of mental functioning is familiar to us. What is not so familiar — outside the esoteric circle of contemplative practitioners of yogic and Buddhist systems of meditation — is the conscious/superconscious distinction. In the field of normal awareness, consciousness is localized and focused; in *samadhi* or higher states of enlightened mind, consciousness is non-local. If one is in three-dimensional space, one can look at the square of a wall or floor, but be aware that one is in the room of the three-dimensional cube. In Dante's Canto 28, and also in Fra Angelico's painting, the Cortona *Annunciation*, the angel cannot fit into the confines of the three-dimensional space of Mary's room or the tight restrictions of linear flowing time. In the case of Fra Angelico's painting, the fall and the redemption are happening simultaneously as facets of a hypersphere crystal. The curve of the angel's wings that stick out of the cube create an arc that infers a larger circle, one that alludes to the circles of the prophet Elijah and the Holy Spirit in the form of a dove that are between the Angel Gabriel and Mary. The clue to the resolution of three-dimensional space and historical time by the phenomenology of the hypersphere is hinted at in the brocade of the material covering Mary's chair, for it shows a two-dimensionally flattened rendering of a torus (see Abraham, in press). In the circulation of movement towards the basin of attraction at the centre of the torus, outside becomes inside and past and future become the sides of the torus, or the wings of the angel. Prebirth and afterdeath are simultaneously present in the hypersphere of — what shall we call it? — hyperconsciousness.

In many ways, humanity does not seem to have taken this artistic rendering of the evolution of consciousness further than in the work of Dante and Fra Angelico. James Joyce, in his *Finnegans Wake*, most certainly did give us a sophisticated biospheric modelling of the 'commodius vicus of recirculation' of conscious and unconscious in the transpersonal life of *Here Comes Everybody*, but he did not present us with the hypersphere of mystical states of *samadhi* or *satchitananda*. Looking around now at our most distinguished English language poets — writers such as John Ashbery or Seamus Heaney — it does not seem as if they or any other poet out there, male or female, is capable of picking up where Dante and Fra Angelico left off. The *genius* of contemporary humanity is wed to technology and not to the hidden god who comes to us by night or poetry and art, so we shall have to wait to see if this marriage is made in heaven — or not.

CHAPTER 2

Speculations on the City and the Evolution of Consciousness

The city is not simply a location in space, but also a vehicle in time that can itself accelerate the evolution of consciousness. Like molecules packed into the membrane of a cell, the minds that are packed into a city take on a new life that is energized by the city's intensification of space and time.

The first cities of ancient Sumer were ceremonial centres organized around the sacred precinct of the temple. Sumerian mythology stated that these cities were founded and lived in by the gods. One of the earliest texts we have in Sumerian mythology is the story of how the goddess Inannna transferred the arts of civilization (the *me*'s) from the god Enki's favoured city of Eridu to her own beloved Erech. The text is a fundamental expression of the ancient Arithmetic Mentality, as it displays the numinosity of the list and delights in repeating, in strophe after strophe, the enumeration of these *me*'s that were loaded on and unloaded from Inanna's riverine barge.

This ancient Sumerian poem, *How Inanna Transferred the Arts of Civilization from Eridu to Erech* (Kramer, 1963, p. 116) enables us to see how both literature and mathematics participate in a historically dependent mentality in which a world-view is structured by a particular dynamical mode of perception and narration, be it Arithmetic (or Ancient), Geometrical (or Classical), Algebraic (or Medieval),

Galilean Dynamical (or Renaissance/Modern), or Chaos Dynamical (or Contemporary).

Within the sacred precinct, a steward, an *Ensi*, ruled over the ceremonial city for the absentee landlord of the god. Over the years, as the gods receded in the daily experience of humans, the day-to-day reality of human rulership became much more visible. We can see this social evolution of mystique into politique as a three-stage process in which the ceremonial centre grows into the imperial city.

1. The gods rule (stage of the *Ensi*)
2. I rule for the gods (stage of shepherd-king)
3. I rule! (stage of the emperor)

Ancient cities around the world seem to begin as ceremonial centres, and then, through trade and warfare, grow into imperial centres. The early Sumerian cities and the Meso-American cities, San Lorenzo Tenochtitlan and Teotihuacan, are examples of the first type. Babylon, Persepolis, Peking and Rome are examples of the second type. From Babylon to Peking to Rome, imperial cities were the general rule for planet Earth during the period of ancient, classical, and medieval civilizations. An empire would rise, extend its rule from court to provinces, until there would be a reversal and the outlying provinces would overrun the imperial city. The climax formation of this civilizational system of a periodic attractor oscillating back and forth between civilization and barbarism was seen in medieval societies like Ming China, pre-Columbian Meso-America, and the Islamic and Christian civilizations surrounding the Mediterranean basin.

In the cultural shift from an empire, based on conquest and tribute, to a polycentric world economy based on trade and finance with interest-generating loans, there arose a shift in perspective from the past to the future. Indebtedness has as its phase-space the future, so one naturally becomes interested in the time to come when one's ship will come in, one's loan will be paid off, and full payment will be made. The new kind of city that arose with this new world economy was the trading city, a Florence, Genoa and Venice at the beginning of the modern period, an Antwerp and Amsterdam in the middle, and a London and New York at the end.

With the expansion of trade and technology, artisans who found themselves in low esteem in aristocratic, feudal societies, found themselves growing in independence and influence as they became the artists and scientists of an expanding industrializing society. A city that grew to become a capital for this new culture of art and science was late-nineteenth-century Paris. Indeed, for the social critic Walter Benjamin, Paris was the capital of Civilization for the last third of the nineteenth century (Benjamin, 1974, pp. 170–84).

For the sake of heuristic playfulness, let us imagine that Paris 1851 to 1914 is a processual object, a phenomenology of culture bounded by a permeable membrane that is reflexive in time and reflective in space. The minds that live within this membrane begin to take on a collective mental behaviour that is peculiar to them, and as they interact within this ethos — or system of values — they begin to bring forth mental creations that seem to flourish within this particular domain of time and space. Like jazz musicians listening to one another's riffs before they take off on their own, Parisians are energizing other Parisians. Manet is listening to Mallarmé at the beginning of this period, and Kupka is listening to Poincaré at the end, but all through this period from 1851 to 1914, all these creative thinkers are listening to Paris. Railways are influencing both Monet and Zola, and as Haussmann's reconstruction of Paris destroyed medieval Paris in order to recreate a more conscious monument to a bourgeois vision of the past, Bergson in *Matière et Mémoire* and Proust in *Du Côté de Chez Swann* also excavated the past in an exploration of the nature of memory as constitutive of human identity. This focussing on matter and its saturation with invested meaning is, of course, not unique to Proust and Bergson, but is at the heart of the capitalistic fixing of value on gold in the new global Gold Standard Economy (Gallarotti, 1995). Interestingly enough, that most unrooted wanderer Rainer Maria Rilke, is also concerned at this time with *Dinglichkeit*, but then Rilke, too, was in Paris and was secretary to Rodin, and Proust was one of the first to read and become enthusiastic about Rilke's poetry. Rilke was also quite influenced by Cézanne, so this new attention to the psychological nature of perception is something worth 'looking at'. When one adds to our thoughts of Manet and Monet, a glance at the beginnings of photography with Marville and Atget, and then with cinema and the brothers Lumières, one begins to appreciate the manner in which city and media are beginning to play off one another.

All of that is not too far out, so let's take it a step further to suggest that what is helping to form the membrane of time and space to give living structure to the evolutionary vehicle of Paris has also to do with an economy as well as a technology, and a war as well as an explosion of artistic and scientific creativity. So let us imagine a table of correspondences:

	Paris	New York	Los Angeles
War:	Franco-Prussian, World War I	World War II	Cold War
Economy:	Gold Standard	'The Crash'	Nixon's post-Breton Woods floating exchange rates — a form of Derrida's 'différance'
Technology:	Railway	Mass transit, Subway and 'El'	Automobile
Media:	Painting, photography and cinema	Radio and movies	Movies and television
Temporal Mode:	The Past, Historical Monument	The Now, Skyscraper	The Future and Fantasy; freeways, theme parks
Dynamical Mentality:	Poincaré	Macy Conferences, Information Theory	Complex Dynamical Systems
Musical Mentality:	Satie	Gershwin, Miles Davis and 'Birth of the Cool'	Music as acoustical architecture, informational economy
Archetypal Novel:	Proust, *A la Recherche ...*	Dos Passos, *Manhattan Transfer*	Pynchon, *Crying of Lot 49*

To take it from the bottom: Satie, from the influence of his mystical Rosicrucian musings of 1891, eliminates temporal markings in his musical compositions and attempts to create a tonal extensiveness, and this is a musical prefiguring of Bergson's 1896 analysis of time as 'durée'. This dissolution of absolute mechanical clock time is echoed in Poincaré's discovery that the solar system is not an orderly mechanical clock, but a chaotic system. Kupka sits in on Poincaré's lectures, and in his paintings from 1911 on he begins to express fractal architectures, self-similarity, and collisions of laminar and chaotic flows (Kolinsky and Andel, 1998). In New York, street sounds in Gershwin and jazz in general begin to explore noise and 'self-organization from noise' right about the time that the scientists in the Macy conferences — Bateson, von Neumann, and von Forster — as well as Shannon across the Hudson in Bell Telephone Labs in New Jersey — are all beginning to study self-organization from noise in cybernetics and information theory. In Los Angeles, the theme park as fake city uses movie music as emotional crowd controls in Disneyland, with speakers in the monorail, the bushes, the lavatories and restaurants.[1] Musak in elevators and factories becomes an experiment with subliminal systems of social control, and pop music expands globally to become a new kind of collective architecture and currency of exchange in the informational economy in which the pop star becomes a new kind of post-industrial tycoon.

In other words, what the moiré pattern of war, economy, media, artistic and scientific invention allows us to see is that minds are not discrete entities but are embedded within an ecology of consciousness, and what the intellectual city like Paris brought forth in its

---

[1] On more than one occasion, younger scholars have accused me of using the ideas of Baudrillard without due citation. My approach to writing on contemporary culture was certainly influenced by Marshall McLuhan, whom I encountered both at MIT and the University of Toronto, but my wrtings on Los Angeles come twenty years before I read Baudrillard. In 1967, I wrote 'Los Angles: Reflections at the Edge of History', which was published in *The Antioch Review* in 1968; it became the first chapter of my book, *At the Edge of History* in 1971. Because this book was nominated for The National Book Award, it was translated into popular editions in French and Italian, where both Baudrillard and Eco could easily encounter it. I went on to write on Disneyland and fake history in the introduction to the 1988 reissue of this book and in my subsequent work, *The American Replacement of Nature* (New York: Doubleday, Currency Books, 1991). I now delight in Baudrillard's outrageously French — and his own arrogantly footnoteless — style, but my approach comes from having grown up in Los Angeles and having been a teenager with a car at the time of the opening of Disneyland.

artistic and scientific creations was the evolution of a new kind of noetic polity of synchronous emergence — one that has now been passed over in new forms of synchronous emergence in more global forms of cyberspace. Paris, as an urban artefact, certainly expressed an escape from nature, but its celebration of the glory of the past with its heroic monuments disguised this shift with a certain conservatism. But with the Eiffel Tower there was a reaching up to break free of nature that inspired New York's efforts to escape the ground of nature in the skyscrapers of the Flatiron Building, the Empire State Building and Rockefeller Center. King Kong falling to his death from the Empire State Building expressed an almost archetypal death of the old nature in the new state of culture.

In Los Angeles, New York's polarization between tenement and penthouse is overcome in the flattened suburban megalopolis of the new postwar universal middle class. Here credit as an imaginary currency becomes the new ground of the economy, and fantasy becomes the new system of identity. The whole culture is literally indebted to the future, so the imagination of the future becomes the new fictional ground that supports value and identity. The great soldiers and scientists of Paris, and the great millionaires of New York, become replaced by the celebrity, a creature of pure image and illusion. In this new State of Entertainment, advertising replaces political philosophy and entertainment replaces education, so a presidential campaign becomes a consensual delusion and Reagan becomes the first Disney animatron president as celebrity, celebrity as president.

Three novels that embody the distinct kairos of their chosen cities are Proust's *À la recherche du temps perdu* for Paris, John Dos Passos' *Manhattan Transfer* for New York, and Thomas Pynchon's *Crying of Lot 49* for Los Angeles. With Proust, perception, memory, and the nature of time are part of a concern that is part of a vast Parisian thought-complex, one shared by Bergson, and the new media of photography and film. With Dos Passos, the writer performs self-consciously modernist fiction in the narrative techniques of collage and quick cuts of simultaneity that focus on the phase-space of the 'now' and prefigure the narrative techniques that have taken over television story-telling, from *Hill Street Blues* to *ER*. With Pynchon, the chaotic informational overload of the megalopolis generates a new landscape of fantasy- identity, conspiracy theories, and paranoid reintegration. Paranoia as a mad system of informational integration is a shadow-formation that paradoxically throws light upon the shift from post-industrial to informational society; it is a caricature of the cultural transition from the world metropolis to the planetary noetic polity in which the territorial nation-state dissolves in visions of globalist associations.

Both nineteenth-century Paris and twentieth-century New York are examples of the city evolving from the materialist and capitalistic city into the informational noetic polity, one in which an overlapping moiré of economic centre, artistic centre, and intellectual centre creates a pattern in which no single institution is imperialistically in control, thus an emergent state comes forth in which consciousness moves to a level above the traditional formations of an urban civilization. Since even this contemporary manifestation of urban form now seems to be simply a node in the planetary informational lattice of the World Wide Web, it is hard to prophesy just where this contemporary noetic polity is taking us in cultural evolution.

My guess is that the etherealization of architecture through atomic nanotechnologies that will enable one to turn buildings on and off like electric lights will make cities like New York nostalgic artefacts, and, just like Haussmann's Paris, historical camouflage to their true but more invisible structure. Los Angeles, in contrast to New York, is a single-industry city, that industry being entertainment — movies, television, and theme parks. Disneyland and Las Vegas are basically theme park suburbs of L.A. From my perspective, L.A. is isomorphic to the Vatican, and is the Vatican of our new State of Entertainment in which politicians, sports figures, movie stars, and celebrities are all the potentates of the new wilfully deluded polity. Cambridge, Mass. is also a single-industry city, and that is what makes it more boring than New York and why creative artists who earn their keep as professors at Harvard, MIT, Tufts, or Boston soon get bored with their unimaginative academic colleagues and move to New York as soon as their income allows them to break loose from tenured servitude to the monocrop noetic polity of the university.

New York is not a single-industry city, and that is what makes it so much more interesting than commercial Zurich, or even contemporary Paris for that matter. Contemporary Paris has more of a conformist and collective manner to its intellectual style of life, but New York is so vast that one can live and write there and never have to run into or conform to the styles of Susan Sontag or Norman Mailer. New York is a kind of mitochondrium of Archaean evolution that has moved into some gigantic Gaian planetary cell for the next stage in evolution. The moiré pattern that emerges from the overlap of

Wall Street, the United Nations, music and performing arts, publishing, and universities makes it now as interesting as Paris must have been in the time of Proust, Bergson and Poincaré.

In the interval between World Wars I and II, the global economy contracted and restructured itself as the capital of the world economy shifted from London to New York. This restructuring is called the Great Depression,[2] and in his efforts to save American capitalism, F.D.R. was not fully successful until he put America on a wartime economy. This extension of credit to the manufacturers was continued through the extension of the war into the Cold War, with its stimulation of the new aerospace industries. This new post-industrial economy was created by massive intrusion of Big Government into the private sector, but almost by accident, in the case of the G. I. Bill, the United States Government stumbled upon the idea of extending credit to the consumers and not just the factory producers, and these new forms of support for higher education and the purchase of homes shaped the new world of the suburbs in the Baby Boom. When the National Defense Act put the construction of the Interstate Highway system also on the federal tab, the wedding of suburban tracts to highways created the new culture of the automobile and the shopping mall. With a continuing extension of credit and indebtedness to consumers, credit cards, television, movies and theme park images of history all interacted to bring forth a whole new post- industrial society.

In his essay 'The Planetization of Mankind' in 1945, Teilhard de Chardin noticed that:

> Every new war, embarked upon by the nations for the purpose of detaching themselves from one another, merely results in their being bound and mingled together in a more inextricable knot. The more we seek to thrust each other away, the more do we interpenetrate (Teilhard de Chardin, 1945, p. 130).

And so after World War II, Detroit automotive factories end up in Japan and Japanese Zen Buddhist monasteries end up in California.

---

[2] Braudel's perception of this shift is brilliant. 'Can one suggest that a highly convenient rule might operate in this context, to wit, that any city which is becoming or has become the centre of a world- economy, is the first place in which the seismic movements of the system show themselves, and subsequently the first to be truly cured of them? If so, it would shed a new light on Black Thursday in Wall Street in 1929, which I am inclined to see as marking the beginning of New York's leadership of the world' (Braudel, 1984, p. 272).

In the countercultural movements of 1968, these Yin and Yang forces collided in America and Western Europe and brought both France and the United States to the edge of civil wars. In industrial society, the displaced agricultural labourers were gathered into factories, looked at one another and recognized themselves as the new working class. In the informational society of the age of television, the young were collectivized in suburbs and public universities, looked around and recognized themselves in the generation gap as the new counterculture. In the War in Vietnam, the United States sought to extend the colonial policies of the French and contain Chinese expansion by controlling Japan's economic dependency on Malaysian and Indonesian oil and resources, and thus the USA expressed the Yang force in a straightforward manner. But the informational proletariat of the young in the US and Western Europe exploded in a new expression of identity, interiority, and mystification of a romantic past in the commune and hippie costume. 'Folk' music was electronically retrieved through the figures of Joan Baez and Bob Dylan, and the Depression of Woody Guthrie became a pastoral artefact in the affluent consumer culture of the sixties.

This first wave of the counterculture of the post-industrial society of the 1960s expressed a revolutionary and Dionysian consciousness in a mystical shift from the territorial nation-state to the 'extraterrestrial' noetic polity, and this found public artistic expression in drugs, global pop music, and many works of popular science fiction concerned with fears of extraterrestrial invasion.

The second wave of the counterculture that came out of Silicon Valley in California in the 1980s expressed a more Apollonian consciousness of re-embodiment in new informational corporations and new forms of Artificial Intelligence. Here we saw a shift from the consciousness of an autonomous self within a biological evolutionary body to more distributive lattices of multidimensional mind in which new media constellated new forms of the extensive phase-space of consciousness through personal computers, the Internet, and the World Wide Web. Thus, in the exchange of opposites that is characteristic of conflict as well as diploid sexual reproduction, the exteriority of the Yang force crosses with the interiority of the Yin force in a form of planetary cellular mitosis that seems about to give birth to a new kind of life in which natural and artificial are more intimately bound together in 'Artificial Life' and electronic organisms.

In this emergence of the novel state of cultural evolution, the old condition is used as a nostalgiac camouflage-content for the structure. Notice that the ideology of capitalism in the United States is filled with the imagery of family values, Evangelical Protestantism, and rugged individualism: all of which are opposite to the cultural drift of the economic processes Republicans energize. In much the same way, Paris in the nineteenth century began by focusing on matter and the past in the photography of Atget, the perspectival monumentality of Haussmann, and the excavations of memory in Bergson and Proust, but ended up in a new non-objective state of consciousness in Poincaré and Kupka, and, of course, in the a-perspectival Cubism of Braque and Picasso. Twentieth century New York started out as an escape from the past into a Modernist Now, but ended up as a hierarchical and highly concretized city as artefact of the corporate past. Postwar Los Angeles started out as the vast extensive and flattened city of the new universal middle class, but ended up as an informational lattice in which nodes such as Las Vegas, Silicon Valley, and Santa Fe became like urban metastases. Our new planetary noetic polity does not seem to be a city fixed to a physical location, so the giantism of Los Angeles now serves as a content- camouflage to its rather monistic uniformity in a consciousness that is locked on to the State of Entertainment, much as New York in the fifties and sixties was locked onto the corporatism of its alluminum and glass skyscrapers around Rockefeller Center.

Before the outbreak of World War I, psychoanalysis, quantum mechanics, cubism, and special relativity began to express an intellectual shift away from the pious certainties of the materialist bourgeois world view. In 1972, a new planetary culture began to express itself in contradistinction to the internationalism that had been dominant in the era of World War II and the Cold War. James Lovelock published his first paper on the Gaia Theory that expressed a new way of looking at planetary dynamics and Jay Forester and the Meadows at MIT published their first efforts at understanding the relationship between the global economy and the global ecology in *Limits to Growth*. New forms of mathematics, first in catastrophe theory and then in chaos dynamics, began to express the shift from linear systems of cause and effect to emergent states and complex dynamical systems. The politics of nation-states are still struggling to understand this cultural transformation in which the interiority of the Yin force expresses itself in the planetization of the esoteric in popular movements of mysticism and meditation, while the Yang force expresses itself in a global economy of GATT and NAFTA. As the ozone hole and the Greenhouse Effect begin to transform global weather patterns, the relationship between the global economy and the global ecology is becoming more apparent, and also, quite apparently, not under the control of the globalist managers. We can call this shift from a collection of competing industrial nation-states to a planetary culture, the shift from a global economy (Clinton, Bush, *et al.*) to a planetary ecumené.

Like the ancient city-states of Sumer that were united by rivers, the new cities along the Pacific Rim seem to be part of an emergent structure that is neither simply a culture nor an economy, but something like the molecular soup that prefigured the evolution of cells. The infectious case of Los Angeles certainly seems to be a model for these new global cities of the Pacific Rim, 'the new Mediterranean'. With more than 80 languages in its public schools, L.A. is no longer simply an 'American' city. It is First World and Third World at the same time.

Perhaps we are experiencing a shift from a world economy of competing and polluting industrial nation-states to a global ecology of noetic polities in which consciousness will become a symbiotic architecture of organisms and machines, one in which pollution is mined as a natural resource in a cultured bacterial technology, and a complex ecology of 'living machines' and electronic organisms (Todd and Todd, 1994). Certainly, to track and describe this new emergent state, we shall need the narratives of complex dynamical systems. Perhaps here science fact and science fiction are coming together to open our imaginations to the future and the possibilities of multidimensional modes of consciousness that can be both mystical and mathematical.

CHAPTER 3

Literary and Archetypal Mathematical Mentalities In the Evolution of Culture

The idea of cultural mentalities first arose in European anthropology's confrontation with global primitive cultures. During the early twentieth century's period of confident imperialism, the European nations articulated their confrontation with non-literate cultures in a poetic imagining of the 'primitive' as a Romantic 'Other'. As psychology developed in Europe to explore the unconscious as well as madness, a new ethnology also sought to enter into the mind of the primitive as an exotic place where logic and reason did not rule.

Lucien Lévy-Bruhl caught the spirit of this time in the first decades of the twentieth century with his *La Mentalité Primitive* (1925), but after the Second World War and the transformation of colonies into independent nation-states, this perspective went out of fashion. It continued for a while in schools of psychology in which the mentality of the child, the primitive, and prehistoric man might be cross-referenced — as they were in Heniz Werner's *Comparative Psychology of Mental Development* (1957) — but it began to fade as Robert Redfield's less judgmental terminology of 'world-view' became more useful in his *The Primitive World and its Transformations* (1953).

At about the time that Lévy-Bruhl's use of the idea of the primitive mentality began to disappear, a new school of French historical thought with *les Annalistes* came forward. Fernand Braudel became its most famous voice, and with his global leadership, the idea of mentality took on a new meaning. To counter the imperial and heroic narratives of traditional history, one in which a Napoleon or a Pasteur figured as a great man advancing the course of human civilization, Braudel put forward the idea of 'the long wave' of history in which ordinary men women with ordinary perceptions looked out at the world in the common mentality of their time. This form of cultural history continues today in the work of such distinguished historians as Carlo Ginzburg.

Michel Foucault, in his archaeology of knowledge, worked to excavate the episteme — the underlying structure that organized different disciplines such as philology and economics in a commonly shared deep structure — but Foucault, in the spirit of the Left of Paris 1968, became focused solely on the idea of power and institutional discourses of power in the asylum and the prison, as these served to illuminate with their darkness the inherent darkness of more accepted institutions of leadership and governance such as the Church, the university, or the state itself. His approach now dominates the postmodernist ethos of most academic departments of literature, and, paradoxically, empowers them to dismiss 'works of genius' as merely patriarchal constructions in the discourse of domination. The capitalist economists who govern our American universities have taken the deconstructing humanists at their word, and now are in the process of deconstructing English as the foundation for a liberal arts education — just as in a previous generation they eliminated Classics as the foundation for a Western Civilization curriculum. For a university's Board of Trustees, the construction of football and basketball facilities provides a greater return on investment in the future donations of the enspirited alumni. The deconstruction of Western Civilization by the very universities funded to preserve it is now complete, and the new planetary civilization will have to look to some new institution or other form of cultural participation to articulate its new values and new world view.

Though radical in his efforts to get at the roots of power and oppression, Foucault, I believe, still did not go deep enough in his archaeology of knowledge; he stayed in the top soil of politics, and did not look at the processual folding of the underlying strata. There is indeed a deep structure that unites a literary narrative and a mathematical algorithm, but it is more based upon the perceptual system of the human body than the body-politic; it is based upon a configuration in which objects are articulated in a constructed space, and a configuration of time, a narrative, in which identities are unfolded. The former is a world, the latter, a self.

Recent research by Lakoff and Núñez has proposed that mathematics is not a Pythagorean or Platonic system dwelling with the Celestial Intelligences and angelic hierarchies, but a system of metaphoric extensions based on the human body.

> Mathematics, as we shall see, layers metaphor upon metaphor. When a single mathematical idea incorporates a dozen or so metaphors, it is the job of the cognitive scientist to tease them apart so as to reveal their underlying cognitive structure.This is a task of inherent scientific interest. But it also can have an important application in the teaching of mathematics. We believe that revealing the cognitive structure of mathematics makes mathematics much more accessible and comprehensible. Because the metaphors are based on common experiences, the mathematical ideas that use them can be understood for the most part in everyday terms (Lakoff & Núñez, 2000, p. 7).

Other recent research has shown that some 'subitizing' mathematical computations arise before spoken language in the child (Dehane, 1997, p. 67), so there is no reason to think that mathematics is a higher order intellectual development that comes only at school age in the socializing institutions that were the focus of attention for Foucault. The metaphoric structure that is at once a positioning of a self in a world and a mathematical operation manipulating objects in an imaginal space, I would propose to term a literary-mathematical mentality. The arising of these mentalities is an emergent domain that is conditioned by the human body embedded within a historical culture and an enveloping cultural-ecology (Thompson, 1985; 1989). As an adaptation to a cultural-ecology, literature behaves ecologically in more ways than one. Like a forest moving through the stages of succession to climax, literature unfolds through three stages: formative, dominant, and climactic. The formative work enters into a new niche of consciousness; the dominant work stabilizes the new mentality — usually through the efficacy of an elite — and the climactic work finishes or completes the possibilities of that now traditional mentality. Generally in history, the almost hieratic crystalization of a mentality is challenged by a new formative work that opens up the possibilities of a whole new mentality — much in

the way that Galileo's work served to initiate a movement from
Catholic theology to modern science.

In human cultural history, I believe that there are five of these
archetypal mathematical mentalities: the Arithmetic Mentality,
which arises in the Ice Age and reaches its climactic formation in
ancient Sumerian civilization; the Geometric mentality which arises
in Egyptian, Akkadian, Indian, Chinese, and Mesoamerican civilizations and reaches its climactic formation in the classical civilizations
of Greece, Rome, India, China, and Mesoamerica; the Algebraic Mentality that arises in ninth century Baghdad and reaches its climax in
the civilization of the Mediterranean cultural-ecology before the Italian Renaissance; the Galilean Dynamical Mentality which arises in
Renaissance Italy and reaches its climactic formation in nineteenth
century Europe; and lastly, the Complex Dynamical Mentality, which
emerges in Paris with Poincaré around 1889 and becomes a conscious
cultural endeavour in places like the Santa Fe Institute in the last
decade of the twentieth century.

Each of these literary-mathematical mentalities can be associated
with a cultural-ecology that historically was inseparable from its
development. And for each of these mentalities embedded in their
characteristic cultural-ecology, there is an archetypal articulation of
objects in space that is the characteristic formation for its world view.
For the Arithmetic Mentality, it is the list: from the list of the arts of
civilization that Inanna transfered from Eridu to Erech in ancient
Sumer to the catalogue of the ships in Homer's *Iliad*. For the Geometrical Mentality, it is the temple. For the Algebraic Mentality, it is the
Esoteric Code. For the Galilean Dynamic Mentality it is the object in
motion, from cannon balls to sailing ships to monetary currencies.
And for the Complex Dynamical Mentality, it is the multi-causal and
synchronous systems in self-organizational emergence — from the
origins of life to consciousness and the ecology of living organisms
that constitute the planetary system of Gaia.

Since Lakoff and Núñez argue that the body is the matrix for the
system of extended metaphors on which mathematics is based, it is
appropriate that cultural historians should now begin to see govern-
ing archetypal mathematical structures as ones that also express
themselves, in theme and structure, in literary and artistic works.
Perhaps primary and secondary schools can now begin to teach
mathematics in the context of the artistic works in which it was
brought forth. Children should learn geometry before algebra, and
should learn it in middle school in the context of the architecture,

sculpture, and history of ancient and classical civilizations. As an effort to correlate these mathematical mentalities with literary works, I offer the following Table.[1]

Cultural Ecology	Mentality	Archetypal Object
Riverine	Arithmetic	The List
Transcontinental	Geometric	The Temple
Mediterranean	Algebraic	The Esoteric Code
Oceanic	Galilean Dynamical	Currencies/Ballistics
Biospheric	Complex Dynamical	Self-Consciousness

The Literary Milestones of the Arithmetic Mentality:

Formative: Sumerian, 'Inanna's Transfer of the Arts of Civilization from Eridu to Erech' (This work shows the archetypal and generative power of the list.)

Dominant: 'Inanna's Descent into the Netherworld' (This work shows the cultural shift from village agriculture to the city-state in which a priestly class develops astronomy as a mythopoeic system of knowledge.)

Climactic: 'The Gilgamesh Cycle', both the Sumerian cycle and the Akkadian epic; Lao Tsu's *Tao Te Ching* (The *Gilgamesh Epic* shows the war of the sexes and the tension between matristic systems of prehistoric authority and charismatic military leadership with its new heroic system of values. The *Tao Te Ching* is the Swan Song for the anarchic, pre-state values of the Eternal Feminine and the creative and generative power of the Tao.)

---

[1] One could also call these mentalities literary-musical-mathematical mentalities. The roots of music go back to the Ice Age, and chant, dance, and song would be performances of the Arithmetic Mentality. The Geometric Mentality arises with Pythagoras and the monochord and the realization of the correspondence between ratio and the length of the string on the monochord. The rise of musical notation is itself a performance of the fascination with a celestial code, and the transcendent qualities of medieval literature are clearly matched in the motets of Machaut. The Galilean Mentality is expressed in the shift from polyphonic to homophonic music, with the almost ballistic arc of the driving force of Beethoven's melodic line. The Complex Dynamic Mentality is very consciously explored by Satie, Cage, or Stockhausen.

The Literary Milestones of the Geometric Mentality:

Formative: The Babylonian Creation Epic, *Enuma Elish*; the Egyptian play 'The Triumph of Horus' (The Babylonian text shows the destruction of the prehistoric Great Mother and the shift to the military patriarchal state. The Egyptian text shows the rise of the power of the Father and dynastic succession with the son and the consequent displacement of power from the mother's brother.)

Dominant: Aeschylus's *Oresteia*; Chinese *Book of Odes* (These texts are supreme examples of the shift from prehistoric blood rituals to rationality, temple formation, and patriarchal succession.)

Climactic: Plato's *Timaeus*; Confucius's *Analects*, The canonized *Old Testament* (These documents become 'classics' and therefore lock in patriarchy and geometrical order as the system of civilization for temple and palace.)

The Literary Milestones of the Algebraic Mentality:

Formative: The *Koran, Wis and Ramin, The Story of Layla and Majnun* (One interesting feature of the shift from the concrete to the abstract is expressed in the shift from sexual love — the kind we see expressed in Horace, Ovid, and Catullus — to romantic love and erotic mysticism. This shift seems to start in India and Persia and soon spreads across Western Europe and reaches a climax in the elaborate behavioral code of Courtly Love in the high middle ages.)

Dominant: *Tristan et Iseult*; *The Quest for the Holy Grail*; *The Death of King Arthur*, Jayadeva's *Gita Govinda* (*The Quest for the Holy Grail* is a prime example in which the concrete landscape becomes an allegorical code, and the lovesongs of Krishna and Radha become dominant guiding works for centuries.) For me the medieval Algebraic Mentality is an algorithmic logical operation that says:

If the daughter does not belong to the father, she belongs to me because I love her. (The Persian poem, *Layla and Majnun*). If the wife does not belong to the husband, then she belongs to me, because I love her. (The Persian *Wis and Ramin*, and the Celtic *Tristan et Iseult*). If God is not a vengeful and frightening Jahweh who belongs only to the Ark, the temple, and the high priest, then God is the Beloved and belongs to me as my heart's desire. (Rumi and Sufism in general.)

Climactic: Dante's *Divine Comedy* (In his 'Letter to Can Grande,' Dante shows how the allegorical mode is transcended by the hermaneutic of the anagogic, and with Dante, Courtly Love becomes Cosmic Love: *'l'amor che muove il sole e l'altre stelle'*.)

The Literary Milestones of the Galilean Dynamical Mentality:

Formative: *Lazarillo de Tormes*; Cervantes's *Don Quixote*; Descartes's *Discourse on Method* (The picaresque narrative celebrates the new non-heroic individualism of the common man, and shows life as a process of learning a new science and wisdom through trial and error.)

Dominant: *Faust* — all versions as performances of the European myth (Faust shows man challenging sacerdotal authority to gain power over nature, which is the domiant scientific myth of modernism. Melville's *Moby Dick* goes back to the *Gilgamesh Epic* in its vision of male-bonding and slaying the beast of nature.)

Climactic: James Joyce's *Ulysses* (A conscious recapitulation of literary history, from the Homeric epic to the modern novel, and a brilliant performance of the shift from the linear narrative of a single hero to the complex dynamical system of an ecology of consciousness — a movement that he develops with *Ulysses* and completes with *Finnegans Wake*.)

The Literary Milestones of the Complex Dynamical Mentality:

Formative: Virginia Woolf, *The Waves*; James Joyce, *Ulysses* and *Finnegans Wake* (We are only in the early stages of this cultural shift, but we saw the shift from text to cinema at the beginning of the twentieth century, and the shift from cinema to electronic media, and the multi-dimensionality of hypertext at the end of the century. God only knows what 'krypton crystals' technology is next.)

Perhaps, a word of caution about the Whig narrative of history as a simple linear process of development is in order here. One mentality is not morally superior to another, and evil can exist at any level. And simply because one bifurcation occurred and brought about a new emergent domain or culture, does not mean that history could only have gone in that direction. I can imagine a culture that might go directly from a geometric and hieroglyphic mentality into a complex dynamical mentality, without going through an alphabetic mentality of radical reductionism, but such imagining takes me in the direction of science fiction and the envisioning of the cultures of other worlds. If one considers the implied presence of the 3-sphere in Dante's angel sphere of Canto 28 in the *Paradiso*, and the possible presence of the 3-sphere in Fra Angelico's painting, the Cortona *Annunciation*, then one can begin to imagine a jump into hyperdimensionality without the turn Western Europe took into a simplistic scientific reductionism (see Abraham, in press).

In the development of the cultural-ecology of the Mediterranean basin, the Algebraic Mentality of Islam influenced the emerging science of Western Europe through the conduits of schools and courts in Palermo and Majorca, and these new ideas passed over into the culture of the Italian Renaissance and helped to bring forth the Galilean Dynamical Mentality. When this Islamic movement from concrete idol to an abstract and invisible divinity rendered into presence through the numinosity of writing interacted with the algorithmic possibilities of the new Indian numerical system, religion, calligraphy, and calculation began to bring about the new emergent domain of the Algebraic Mentality. Ideographic and hieroglyphic thinking can bring forth the celestial complexity of pattern, but it remains a baroque elaboration of the Geometrical Mentality. Harold Innis and Marshall McLuhan of the Toronto school of communications theory maintained that alphabetic thinking — as a radical move toward simplification and abstraction — gave rise to representational government and western scientific thinking. Certainly, it is hard to imagine the Algebraic Mentality coming forth without this shift. Indeed, in Marcia Ascher's new study of 'Mathematics Elsewhere', divination systems can be seen to be magical squares and binary patterns — patterns characteristic of the Geometrical Mentality — but when Islamic influence and Arabic script meet these African systems in Madagascar, then 'a multistep algebraic algorithm is followed' (see Ascher, 2002, pp. 14–15).

Sacred calligraphy is the apotheosis of writing and it could not have emerged without the Semitic prophetic tradition in which Moses received the written commandments on Sinai, and Mohammed received the sacred dictation of the *Koran* from the archangel Gabriel.

I believe it is this Islamic shift away from concrete pagan idols to a transcendental and invisible Allah whose compassion for mankind is registered in an angelic script that is the cultural matrix out of which algebra emerges. Classical geometry had been a mentality concerned with the order of the seen: the innudations of the banks of the Nile that erased the previous season's farms and so called for remeasurement, as well as the measurements necessary for the constructions of the temples of a ceremonial center. Algebra is an empowerment of the transcendental and invisible through the medium of a celestial code. Calligraphy is a performance of reverence for this code. When the Aramaic alphabetic miniaturization of language was transformed into the Indian numeral system, a new lightness and portability of mathematical operations was made possible through the numinosity of a sacred script.

The notion that behind visible nature is a unifying angelic code that can lead to wisdom and illumination is the step that the genius of Islam set into motion in the Mediterranean cultural-ecology. To be sure, scholars now can show how deeply embedded the *Koran* is in Aramaic texts and earlier Semitic traditions such as are expressed in the *Book of Enoch*,[2] and the peace of the world would be well served if we all celebrated the closeness of the Abrahamic religions, but it is the expansion of Islamic civilization — from Persia to Sicily and Iberia — that carries this new mentality to Western Europe. As biblical and Koranic exegesis develops into a hermeneutical way of looking at the world, mediaeval allegory becomes the celebration of the code over the concrete. And as alchemy develops in Egypt and spreads to the West, it establishes a notation of emblematic books with secret meanings for initiates only. The sunset-effect of this medieval tradition will linger on into the Renaissance and find its final expression in the emblematic books of Robert Fludd and Athanasius Kircher. As the mechanization of writing took over in the printed books of what McLuhan called 'The Guttenberg Galaxy', the entrancement with a celestial code compressed into Rosicrucianism, and the new mathematical mentality shifted away from the esoteric and invisible to the exoteric and visible world of falling bodies for Galileo, circling planets for Kepler and Newton, and ballistic projectiles for Leibniz.

The mechanization of script with print, and the mechanization of time with public clocks proved difficult to those committed to the genius of Islam. Calligraphy was a sublime art that could exalt one's consciousness to the divine. The call to prayer was a human experience sounded by a human voice and not an event produced by iron and brass turned by gears and struck by hammers.[3]

This new literary-mathematical mentality of Renaissance Europe was one in which motion generates value. The motion of sailing vessels produces a new world and a new conception of the world-space. The motion of money through time produces interest with its growth of capital — and one needs to remember that for the mediaeval mentality of both Catholic and Muslim, interest is *usura* and is evil. The motion of the blood in Harvey's new theories of cir-

---

[2]   See Alexander Stille's comments on the scholarship of Christoph Luxenberg in Germany in Stille (2002).

[3]   'They hold that their scriptures, that is, their sacred books, would no longer be sacred if they were printed' (see Lewis, 2002, p. 118).

culation shifts the emphasis for modern medicine from the humours of the liver and spleen to the pulse of the more dynamic heart. The motion of the heavenly bodies in the works of Copernicus, Kepler, Galileo and Newton produces a new physics and system of scientific laws. The motion of cannonballs destroys medieval fortifications — most dramatically with the fall of Byzantium in 1453 — and brings forth a new system of strategic power for kingdoms that will transform themselves into industrial nation-states. And the motion of the individual out of his class produces a new system of personal identity in a rags to riches picaresque narrative in which feudal tradition can no longer hold the person in place. The heroic epic has its last flourish in the sunset-effect of Ariosto's *Orlando Furioso*, but in lamenting the end of the age of knightly chivalry, Cervantes gives birth to the modern novel with its epistemological concerns about the nature of appearance and reality.

Lest one think that literary-mathematical mentalities need only be the concern of the academic cultural historian, consider the following turning point in world political history. From 1405 to 1433, Zheng He, a Mongolian Muslim and Chief Eunuch of the Chinese Emperor Yong Le, served as an admiral of a vast armada of ships — ships so large that they displaced 1600 tons and were 450 feet long. Zheng sailed to India and to Africa, and recently some scholars have begun to claim that he even skirted Antarctica and made it to Brazil. The Admiral went in search of tribute for the Emperor, and had he received as much commitment from the Imperial Court as the space programme did from President Kennedy, China would have become the world power. From the Silk Road to the sea routes, this civilization — at that time the world's greatest — would have projected to form our global civilization, and we would all be speaking Chinese instead of English. But the Confucian court was completely dominated by a geometrical mentality in which all value was at the centre and all inferiority lay with the foreigners at the periphery. They demanded that the costly expense for these expeditions be halted; the courtiers also insisted that the capital move inward from coastal Nanking to Peking, and so the Ming Dynasty retreated and locked itself up in an Imperial court that was, in effect, a rigid crystalization of the classical geometrical mentality. For the realm of space, all value was seen to reside at the centre in the imperial court with its Mandate from Heaven, and for the realm of time, all value derived from the past in a fixed and unchanging Confucian system of patriarchy and ancestor worship. This conservative attitude in which all control is locked to a single center still influences contemporary Chinese modes of governance, and is reflected in the ruling elite's inability to deal with an independent Tibet, Hong Kong, or Taiwan.

But if the expansion of the Islamic algebraic mentality coming round the coast of Northern Africa had met up with this Mongolian-Islamic expansion coming up the coast of South Africa, and, perhaps, even across from Brazil, our world civilization would have been completely different. As it turned out, Islamic science filtered into Europe through Sicily and Iberia — through the court of Richard II in Palermo and the school for the conversion of the heathen Muslims with Ramon Lull on Majorca. But translation of pagan and heathen documents also influenced the faithful Christians, and Islamic navigation maps may very well have ended up in Christopher Columbus' hands — or, at least, rumours of what other sailors had seen and passed on by word of mouth to members of their calling. In short, it was the Islamic algebraic mentality that laid the foundations for the Italian Renaissance and Western Science, and Western Europe could not have passed so easily into the new era without its assistance and cultural transformation. Ironically, it was an early case of Islamic fundamentalism that began to shut down the genius of Islamic science, forcing all scientists to conform to holy writ rather than experiment. But then, these challenges to periods of Enlightenment come and go, and return, as even now Christian fundamentalists work hard to take over local school boards so that they can insist that the textbooks that favour Darwin and evolutionary biology not be used, but in their stead ones that favour the kind of rural folklore they call creationist science (see Turner, 1995, p. 226).

1889 is the magic year for the emergence of the new Complex Dynamical Mentality, for that is the year Poincaré discovers the homoclinic tangle (or the three body problem in physics) and discovers that the solar system is not the orderly eliptical system of Kepler, but a chaotic system. 1889 is as well a good year to date the emergence of a new planetary culture through the agency of 'the City of Light', because that was the year of the Universal Exhibition in Paris, for which the Eiffel Tower was created. For the first time in history, a man-made structure was higher than the Great Pyramid. And it was at this Universal Exhibition that global music was born and Satie first heard the Gammalan music of Indonesia. Satie was so impressed with its rhythms, that he rethought his whole notion of time as a linear succession of units of quantitative time — a tyranny of the mechanization of time that had marked Western music and become policed by the little machine of the metronome. And at the time that Satie was rethinking the quality of time as qualitative durée, so were Bergson and Proust in their parallel researches into the nature of memory and the construction of human time in the field of consciousness.

Proust grew up in the era of Haussmann's appropriation of Paris for the new and costly apartment houses of the expanding and affluent upper-middle class. Baron Haussmann destroyed the actual gritty, dark, and smelly mediaeval past of the Left Bank and eastern Paris to create a new and imaginary Paris of open spaces with perspectival sight-lines for constructed monuments to France's glorious past, and broad boulevards for the *flâneurs* of the time (see Jordan, 1995). In fact, Haussmann started the fabrication of the past and initiated the political process of what would become the theme park versions of patriotic American history that Disney created for Disneyland and Disneyworld. How appropriate that Europe's first Disneyland should be placed near Paris!

But Proust's nostalgia for memory and past time attracted him to the vanishing world of the aristocracy as a trope for the vanishing of all human tradition in the face of the contemporary transformation of culture. Like the literary critic Walter Benjamin's vision of the angel of progress that faces backwards against the future into which it moves, Proust looked back to capture past time, but chose the wrong people to mark the passing of his own unique time in world cultural history. As Marshall McLuhan said, 'the sloughed-off environment becomes a work of art in the new and invisible environment.' What was visible to Proust was the wealth of *La Belle Epoque* and the pre-war glory of the Gold Standard world economy (see Gallarotti, 1995). What was invisible to him was the noetic polity in which art and science were creating a new emergent domain in human culture. It was not at aristocratic dinner parties at the palatial homes of the Duke and Duchess of Guermantes that Paris was to transform world civilization. Rather, it was in the parallel processing of art and science that Paris brought forth — not a trading city like London or Venice before it — but an intellectual capital, one so brilliant in its gathering of poets, painters, mathematicians, and scientists that the critic Walter Benjamin (1974) called Paris 'the capital of the nineteenth century'.[4]

So let us date the emergence of planetary culture with this year of 1889. Poincaré's works would influence Einstein, Picasso and Kupka, and they would also initiate new directions in the mathematics that followed with the catastrophe theory of René Thom's work in the 1960s in Paris, the Chaos Dynamics of the 70s and 80s in the United States, and the foundation of the Santa Fe Institute for the Sciences of Complexity in the 1990s. What had been only an idea in the mind of a mathematical genius in 1889 was a new global scientific culture by 1989.

At the time of Poincaré, Frantisek Kupka (1871–1957), a Czech painter was also working in Paris and attending lectures at the Sorbonne, where Poincaré was a popular lecturer. Kupka painted images very similar to fractals as early as 1910, and broke with cubism to explore the collisions of laminar and chaotic flows. Also during this period in Paris, chaos appeared in Erik Satie's surrealist ballet *Parade* (1917). Paris, the avant garde's leading edge, was 'where it was at', and writers from provincial backwaters like Ireland or the American Midwest — writers as different as James Joyce, F. Scot Fitgerald, Gertrude Stein and Ernest Hemingway — all would be drawn to Paris in order to take part in the great transformation of civilization that they could sense and express in art but not explain in the common ideas of their day. No one could say in 1889, as we can now, with the benefit of 20/20 hindsight, that they were experiencing the cultural transition from the modern industrial nation-state to the noetic polity, but they could feel that something new in human cultural evolution was happening, and that Paris was the place to be to experience it. It was this new avant garde experience of participating in a new culture through a heightened sense of consciousness that was the defining characteristic of life in a noetic polity. Before, cultural transformations were too long and a human life too short for the individual to know he or she was living in a new cognitive domain, but the mutual interactions of art and science in the modernist movement served to make this cultural transforma-

---

[4] Surprisingly, Patrice Higonnet (2002) misses the significance of Poincaré and chooses the year 1889 to mark the end of the mythic era of Paris. His point of view is too narrowly political and literary, and a much more sensitive understanding of the importance of science to art is to be found in Miller (2001); see especially his Chapter Four, 'How Picasso Discovered *Les Desmoiselles d'Avignon*'.

tion visible. This transition from nation-state to noetic polity was not simply the creation of the university. Just as the College of Cardinals did not create the Italian Renaissance, or Oxford and Cambridge bring forth the evolutionary theories of Wallace, Darwin and Huxley, but, instead, became the seat of smug opposition to them, so did this tremendous intellectual revolution not come exclusively from the university. The campus was Paris; it included the Sorbonne, yes, but also the cafés, streets, galleries and concert halls of this exciting city. It was the crossing of art and science that created the moiré pattern of a noetic community that was neither simply scientific nor exclusively artistic.

The play of the imagination was wilder and more free than academe can ever tolerate, and in this context, it is interesting to note just how important the occult and the esoteric that always offend the sensibilities of academics were in the creative process of articulating a new mentality beyond the accepted forms of what Whitehead called Scientific Materialism. Both X-rays and Theosophy helped to establish an appreciation for the invisible. Theosophy was important to Kandinsky, to Kupka, to Mondrian, to Yeats, and Rosicrucianism was important to Satie. 'The New Age' is really not all that new.

Whether this emergence of planetary culture can continue to come forth, or whether we slide down into a Dark Age that could last for centuries, depends now on just how quickly humanity can evolve beyond the level of warring religions, techno-idolatry and deterministic science to the new post-religious spirituality and science that was prefigured by Einstein and the time of genius of the noetic polity of Paris — a time that was followed by all the wars of the political ideologies of the twentieth century and the wars of religion of the twenty-first. To halt this too easy slide into a Dark Age, we need to set aside the academic 'culture wars' of Eurocentric versus Afrocentric and give thanks for what humanity was given by the geniuses of the City of Light when the new mentality illuminated the transition from the nation-state to the noetic polity.

All cultures are not the same, and in his latest work the theorist on the evolution of consciousness, Merlin Donald, has warned us against slipping into the facile cultural relativism of postmodernist movements in education.

> The extreme forms of cultural relativism that have dominated so many academic disciplines in recent years have completely missed the point. Cultural relativism makes no sense in the cognitive domain, in view of

the fact that cultural differences become manifest as very deep cognitive differences (Donald, 2001, p. 213).

It is easier to smash a Stradivarius than to build one, just as it is easier to hijack an airplane than design and build it, so humanity will need to realize now that neither religions, nation-states, nor machines can serve any longer as the appropriate vehicles for human cultural evolution. Each of the mentalities of the past has had its appropriate educational institution to bring forth the new mentality, from the temple to the Pythagorean Academy to the House of Wisdom in Al Kwarizmi's Baghdad to the modern scientific and technical university. Now a new institution will have to be created to embody and foster the new planetary civilization. My generation did what it could within the political limitations imposed by the commercial materialism, academic nihilism, and religious fanaticism of our time; but the countercultural institutions such as Esalen or my own Lindisfarne Association were more like crocuses signaling a change of season in early March than they were the hardy trees that could withstand a blizzard in April or a new climate.

The world will most likely have to wait until this current war between the two noetic plasmas of globalization and Islamicist nativistic revolt — culturally diffuse forms that are struggling to become true noetic polities beyond the bourgeois form of the industrial nation-state — have played out whatever fate they have in store for the capitalistic European civilization that projected in the fifteenth century. Indeed, the new triumvirate of Cheney, Rumsfeld and Bush Junior is providing us with such a reductionist caricature of 'The Protestant Ethic and the Spirit of Capitalism' that the United States may serve to so reduce the West as to end it and its global projection of the era from 1453 to 2003. And even our contemporary Anglo-American intellectual culture is itself split and now splitting off from Europe: as one part of it is entranced with extreme reduction- ism and eliminativism — as, for example, in the cognitive science of the Churchlands, the philosophy of Dan Dennett, and the biology of Richard Dawkins — while another part, one more based on the continental philosophies of thinkers like Jean Gebser or Francisco Varela, is labouring to articulate the vision of a new kind of Integral Science.[5] If global civilization gets out of this present conflict alive, then Western Civilization will have transformed itself into a

[5] Each generation has its own way of passing on its spiritual genes to the children and grandchildren. When Lindisfarne began its gatherings in the seventies — ones that carried on into the nineties — there were older people present who

planetary culture in a new way of knowing the universe in which the Orphic and Pythagorean streams reconnected to rush forward in a stronger river toward a greater sea.

had been part of Bauhaus and the Macy conferences, and even one person who had been in the room when Virginia Woolf gave her legendary talk about 'A Room of One's Own'. Along with the scientists Gregory Bateson, Heinz von Forster, James Lovelock, Humberto Maturana, Francisco Varela, Lynn Margulis, Heinz and Elaine Pagels, Arthur Zajonc, Amory Lovins, John Todd, Wes Jackson, Ralph Abraham, Stuart Kauffman, Tim Kennedy, Luigi Luisi, and the astronaut Rusty Schweickart, there were the poets Gary Snyder, Wendell Berry, and Kathleen Raine, the architects Sim Van der Ryn and Paolo Soleri, the Jazz musician Paul Winter, the English painter Haydn Stubbing, Governor Jerry Brown, UN Under-Secretary Maurice Strong, the social and political scientists Mary Catherine Bateson, Hazel Henderson, Richard Falk, and Saul Mendlovitz, and a healthy assortment of non-scientific mystics that included Hopi Elders, Zen Masters, Tibetan Rinpoches, Sufis, Yogis, Cabbalistic rabbis, Quakers, Episcopal bishops and deans, and a Benedictine monk. Our parallel processing of art and science sought to take a third step, one in which we brought practising contemplatives from all the major traditions into the conversations with artists and scientists, because I felt that these esoteric practices were the appropriate miniaturizations of the world's religions that could serve as the ancient mitochondrial DNA within the new larger cell of Gaian planetization. So for the last twenty-five years of the twentieth century, the Lindisfarne Association reached back to the generation of Gregory Bateson and the Macy Conferences, and forward to pass the torch to a new generation of neuro- and cognitive scientists like Tim Kennedy and Evan Thompson. What the café had been for turn of the century Paris, the Lindisfarne Conferences became for our generation: an intellectual chamber music ensemble giving a performance of a noetic polity seeking to be born in the interval between Viet Nam and 9/11.

CHAPTER 4

The Borg Or Borges?

Reflections on Machine Consciousness

It is a paradox of the work of Artificial Intelligence that in order to grant consciousness to machines, the engineers first labor to subtract it from humans, as they work to foist upon philosophers a caricature of consciousness in the digital switches of weights and gates in neural nets. As the caricature goes into public circulation with the help of the media, it becomes an acceptable counterfeit currency, and the humanistic philosopher of mind soon finds himself replaced by the robotics scientist.

What is common to most of the practitioners in the new field of A.I. or Machine Consciousness is a preliminary move that eliminates the phenomenon one wishes to explore and then goes on to celebrate the scientific power of the engineer's new academic discipline. Sloman and Chrisley show this eagerness to move away from the phenomenon of consciousness so as to feel more adequate with the tools and concepts of one's discipline. 'We start with the tentative hypothesis that although the word 'consciousness has no well-defined meaning, it is used to refer to aspects of human and animal information processing'. This is equivalent to saying that dimensionality has no well-defined meaning, so let us define a cube as a set of lines. In a similar move of eliminativism, Susan Blackmore defines consciousness as an illusion generated by competing memes, but this confident Dawkinsian proclamation is as silly as saying that sunshine is an illusion generated by competing leaves.

This atmospheric inversion from above to below, one in which a sky turns into the smog of a thickened air, happened once before in the world of knowledge, when Comtian positivism inspired a functionalist approach to the study of the sacred. The social scientists first said that in order to study the sacred, one had to study how it functioned in society; then having contributed to the growth of their own academic domain, they more confidently claimed that what humans worshipped with the sacred was, in fact, their own society. There simply was no such thing as God or the sacred, and so Schools of Divinity began to be eclipsed by the elevation of the new towers of the office buildings of the Social Sciences. Indeed, as I turn now away from my computer screen, I can see outside my window, the William James Building of Social Relations competing for dominance of the skyline with the Victorian brick Gothic of Harvard's Memorial Hall.

This clever move to eliminate the phenomenological reality of human consciousness as a prelude to the growth of a new robotics industry is a very successful scam, for it has helped enormously with the task of fund-raising for costly moon shots, such as the Japanese government's 'Fifth Generation Computer Project' which promised to create an autonomously thinking machine in the 1980s. No one seems to talk much anymore about the failure of this project, but the gurus of A.I. continue to prophesy — as Ray Kurzweil now does — that by 2030, humans will be surpassed by machines in cultural evolution.

Both the mechanists and the mystics say that we are now at a great bifurcation in human evolution. The mechanists like Ray Kurzweil, Danny Hillis, and Hans Moravec prophesy that we are at the end of the human era, and that 'nanobots' are about to be embedded in our bodies until our antique organs of flesh are entirely surrounded by a new silicon noosphere of networked computers.[1] Like ancient mitochondria or chloroplasts surrounded by the gigantic eukaryotic cell, we are about to be engulphed in the next evolutionary stage. So the mechanists see noetic technologies surrounding human culture and consciousness and compressing it into an endosymbiont in a larger and swifter and more elegant evolutionary vehicle.

Technologists are closer to paranoids than they are to mystics in the sense that they are literalists given to perceptions of misplaced concreteness; they always see spiritual experiences as the products of technology — as emergent domains that are caused by technological innovations, such as LSD or computer networks. The 'difference

---

[1] See Ray Kurzweil, EDGE [Internet Magazine], March 25, 2002; see also his *The Age of Spiritual Machines* (New York: Viking, 1999). Also Hans Moravec, *Mind Children: the Future of Robot and Human Intelligence* (Cambridge, MA: Harvard University Press, 1988).

that makes a difference' — in the famous phrase of Gregory Bateson — between the mystic and the paranoid is that the mystic is in a state of wild cognitive and creative joy, the *satchitananda* of the yogi, but the paranoid is in a condition of anxiety and a cosmic sense of disorientation to the world of spirit that forces him or her into a fixation on literalism and the control of reality through machines. Rather than saying her spiritual intuition has inspired her to see a pattern of connectedness to a world of higher dimensions, s/he claims to have been abducted by flying saucers who have implanted microchips into her head and are beaming directly into her brain from the mother ship.

Mystics flip this literalism over to see technology as a system of externalized metaphors that derive from pre-existing ontological modes at play and at large in the universe. For them, technology is like the Catholic Baltimore Catechism's definition of a sacrament: 'an outward sign of an inward state'. For the mystic — be she Cabbalist or Sufi — an angel is a 'Celestial Intelligence', a form of cosmic noetic organization that does not require a detour through animal evolution. So when Kurzweil claims that by 2030 implanted nanobots in the bloodstream will enable humans to turn off to the outside world to attune to a virtual reality, the mystic would recognize a literalist rendering of the process of meditation. Kurzweil's vision of the world in 2030 reminds me of Borges's 'Library of Babel'. 'I suspect that the human species — the unique species — is about to be extinguished, but the Library will endure: illuminated, solitary, useless, incorruptible, secret'.[2] And here we need to be sensitive to the full force of Borges's use of the word 'Babel'.

The mystics, starting with Teilhard de Chardin and Sri Aurobindo in the first half of the twentieth century, also prophesied that we were at a new stage in evolution, but they saw consciousness surrounding technology, and compressing and miniaturizing it into an antique fossil of intermediate cultural evolution as we passed on into a posthuman or 'Supramental' era in which we were welcomed back into the cosmic play.

In the eight intensive dimensions that String Theory claims are infolded into the three dimensions of extension and the single dimension of linear time, we now can see that there is more room for humans to think in than we thought we had during the age of 'the

---

[2]   Jorge Luis Borges, 'The Library of Babel' in *Labyrinths* (New York: New Directions, 1962), p. 58.

conquest of space'. So what Kurzweil conceives of as only possible through the concretization of a machine may actually be possible through a heightened sensitivity to other noetic dimensions. Kurzweil would like the computer to be for him what the organ was to Bach: a way of releasing the human mind into the larger Mind of the universe.

For the mechanists, the flesh is slow, sloppy, and wet, and, therefore, primitive. For the Christian mystics, the flesh is the body and blood of the living God. Slow and wet is the ontology of birth and the act of making love. Because the neurons are embedded in an aquaeous solution, even distant neurons can participate in a neuronal synchrony through vibrating in the musical harmonies of a single thought. Because the forty Hertz of this neuronal synchrony is slow compared to a silicon computer, it can orchestrate unplanned synchronies in acts of surprise, discovery, analogy, imagination, and metaphoric play. Fast is fine for the programmed crystaline world of no surprises and no discoveries, but slow is better for the creative world of erotic and intellectual play.

If one speeds up a Beethoven string quartet, one may enhance the baud rate of data-processing, but one will no longer have music. In fact, with the increase in speed one has lost consciousness of the work. A Beethoven string quartet is, indeed, a rather sophisticated exploration of the nature of time and consciousness, and the interaction between the different instruments is an artistic recapitulation of the evolutionary development of the nervous system in which different channels of information had to be held over in time and cross-referenced with one another to form an 'I'. In Beethoven's 16th Quartet, the third movement, with the markings of *'Lento assai, e cantante tranquillo'* is so slow as to hover at the very edge of melody and silence. Instead of looking to digital computers as a source for metaphors of mind, it would be more instructive to look, or listen, to music. In Kurzweil's emphasis on speed as the unique excellence of mind, he has lived up to his German name too literally, and so, paradoxically, become *langweilig*. The field of consciousness has more to do with slowness and a higher dimensionality, even beyond the three of the physical volume of the brain, in which hyperspheres — or some other higher dimensional topology — involve simultaneity in a neuronal synchrony — in a pattern. A mind, in the opening words of Keats's 'Ode on a Grecian Urn', is a 'still unravished bride of quietness', a 'foster-child of silence and slow time'.

Slowness is fundamental to the nature of consciousness, and here I would define consciousness as the phase-space of the perceptual-motor system. I would argue that in the evolution of consciousness, as far back as the spirochete, it was the delay-space between two different channels of sensory registry, say between light and dark, on the one hand, and acid or base — or a glucose gradient — on the other, that enabled the molecularly lingering traces to be cross-referenced with one another in the formation of an interpretative domain, such as 'Danger!' or 'Flee!'[3] One channel of sensory registration can be a digital gate, a matter of plus or minus, but when two or three differing sensory registrations are cross-referenced to one another, an emergent domain is brought forth. We move up to a new meta-level — like lines forming the higher dimensionality of a cube or hypercube. An interpretive domain is a subjective experience of a sentient being that can suffer precisely because it has an identity, and is thus, quite literally, identifying with its sensory registrations in an experiential interpretation of its ontological condition, its life. The neuroscientist Francisco Varela liked to use the Buddhist concept of 'grasping' to mark this aspect of a being identifying so totally with its sensory registrations. As multiple channels of sensory registration develop, a network develops that stabilizes the delay-space, and this is its central nervous system. The natural history of an organism's structural coupling with its environment expresses a reinforcing pattern of response, and this stable response is its identity, its fundamental stabilization of time, its egohood, or, at least, its fundamental *Eigenheit*. If these autonomous identities reproduce themselves with heritable variation over time, we call this evolution.

An engineer can be clever and construct a machine that says 'Ouch!' instead of flashing a red light, but this gnostic demiurge is mimicking consciousness to trick humans. The machine is not a sentient being capable of suffering, and, by imaginative extension and recapitulation of suffering, capable of experiencing compassion for the suffering of other sentient beings.

The mechanists are still not free of the mentality of Galilean Dynamics with its linear system of single causal reductionism. This kind of causal narrative is especially characteristic of the school of

[3] I argue this point at greater length in my chapter 'The Past Evolution of Consciousness; from Spirochete to Spinal Chord' in *Coming into Being: Artifacts and Texts in the Evolution of Consciousness* (New York; St. Martin's Press, 1996; 1998), pp. 17-44.

Eliminativism of Paul and Patricia Churchland. The simple and linear binary gates of 1 and 0 are fine for artificial neuronal nets and weights, but if one wishes to enfold complexity and make it portable for the life of a unique individual, then the sloppy and chaotic folding of proteins in a cell or of neurons in a brain is the way to go. The brain is actually the most complex small structure we know of in the universe. Like the Borg of *Star Trek,* the mechanists have perverted evolution, for it is the wet and the biological that is the truly advanced design, and our clunky and rigid metalo-plastic computers are the primtive idols of our literal-minded American technoculture. So I side with the mystics and think that the mechanists are caught in the boomerism of American hypercapitalism and are simply hawking their wares.

In this unreflective boomerism of American hypercapitalism, one has to hype one's project to attract venture capital. If one begins to discuss the possible side-effects of the invention, the shadow-side of the design, or the complexity that is the deep background to the object that is being foregrounded, then the investors head for the exits, afraid of law suits. Ironically, this process of self-deception and faulty design only increases the likelihood of lawsuits, for all products have unforeseen side-effects. In our American rush to production and marketing, we take a protein out of context, a gene out of context, a cell out of context, a plant out of an ecology, and a brain out of the context of its complete body incarnation, and we seek ways to sell drugs, genes, patented plants, organs, and soon, perhaps, entire beings. Perhaps Monsanto and Microsoft and Disney will soon be able to effect a merger that will enable them to patent cultures and EPCOT can take it to the next level. Or could it be that this hostile takeover of culture is what is truly frightening the Muslim world?

The simultaneous fascination and repulsion of Islamic culture to American techno-idolatry is not surprising. Whenever there is a new emergent state of being in the transformations of culture, all of humanity does not immediately shift to the new mentality. If a space voyager wandered around Italy in the fifteenth century, seeking to interview people concerning their excitement at being alive at the time of the Italian Renaissance, most people would not know what the interviewer was talking about. They were still living in the Middle Ages, and would continue to do so until their death.

And so it is now, for most scientists and businessmen are not aware of the implications of complex dynamical systems or of the cultural shift from modernism and the industrial nation-state to planetary culture. So when I am writing about the emergence of a new post-religious spirituality that is in resonance with science — as foreshadowed in such figures as Einstein — I am perfectly aware that I am living in the 'sunset-effect' time of Osama bin Laden and Jerry Fallwell, and that for the billions alive at this moment, their commitment to religion is not about to disappear any time soon. Actually, things need not always disappear in evolutionary extinctions, they can just become surrounded by a new envelopment that is invisible to them. The anaerobic bacteria in my guts are still doing their thing, just as they did billions of years ago before the new atmosphere of oxygen sent them scurrying into the comforts of the dark.

For example, one implication of complex dynamical systems for capitalism is a new version of Adam Smith's 'invisible hand' in which bottom-up causation replaces top down controls.[4] Both socialism and monolithic corporate capitalism are top-down systems of control that seek to monopolize markets and control governments through lobbying, donations, and control of the media. This form of old capitalism is intimately conjoined to modernism, the emergence of the middle class nation-state, and the Galilean Dynamical Mentality. The new capitalism could be a more synergistic system of mutual wealth generation in which groups of inventors bring forth a new cultural-ecology. It is a vision of the World Wide Web and the Internet that is more in tune with Linux than Microsoft. Now just as the Inquisition and the Counter Reformation sought to block the Renaissance, so these gigantic corporations like Microsoft or Monsanto are seeking to block the planetary renaissance and this new possibility for capitalism by maintaining the dualistic systems of the domains of the extremely rich and the extremely poor. Microsoft wishes to own the new cultural-ecology of the noosphere, and Monsanto, and other companies, are seeking to own the genome of plants, animals, and humans. We may slide into a dark age of religious violence with multinational corporations functioning as a tribal amphictyony of competing war lords so that our emergence to an enlightened planetary culture may have to wait a century or two. The Medicis of the Italian Renaissance started out as a merchant class, but they ended up as an aristocracy in the gaudy displays of

[4] For an explanation of emergent properties and bottom-up causation in cognitive science, see Evan Thompson & Francisco Varela, 'Radical embodiment: neural dynamics and consciousness', *Trends In Cognitive Sciences* 5 (2001): 418-425.

wealth so characteristic of the baroque economy that was based upon African slavery. The spiritual opening of the Italian Renaissance became blocked by the Inquistion, the Counter Reformation, and the Age of Absolutism. Humanity had to wait until the eighteenth century for the Age of Revolution to pick up where the Italian Renaissance left off. But if we are lucky, the new form of middle class capitalism that is wed to information technologies and complex dynamical systems may outcompete the recidivist capitalism of the plantations of Monsanto and Microsoft.

At the moment, however, it does not look good, as President Bush et alia are wedding imperial capitalism to Christian fundamentalism with its repression of complexity in the arts and sciences in a state of permanent war against terrorists, first foreign, but soon domestic. As Ashcroft has said, carrying on in the tradition of J. Edgar Hoover and Senator McCarthy, those who would restrain him with their misguided liberal notions are 'only giving ammunition to the enemy'.

The boomerism of hypercapitalism that we see expressed in Kurzweil's millenarian vision of the technological replacement of humanity can be easily hitched to Cheney and Rumsfeld's corporate agenda to surround and contain humanity in a perfect system of high tech defense. Here it might help to recall that the high philosophic science of Heisenberg and von Weizsäcker joined in with the corporate agenda of I. G. Farben to assist in National Socialism's drive to defeat Bolshevism. And E. O. Wilson's consilient campaign to unify all the sciences also comes at a timely moment to help the Right Wing's desire to eliminate 'secular humanism'.[5] By eliminating philosophical divergence and the distinct cognitive approaches of different disciplines, Wilson's ideological program of elitist unification would serve to remove the humanities and their tradition of liberal humanism in a new scientific version of a Talibanic state of consilient unity. Total explanations soon become totalitarian states. Dissent can be labeled depression and ministered to by the contributions of the pharmaceutical industry. With Ritalin in the schools, Prozac in the universities, Zoloft in the prisons, Ecstasy in the discos, and Viagra in the Senate, America can indeed be at peace with itself to let Kurzweil's machines inherit the Earth.

---

[5]   E. O. Wilson, *Consilience: the Unity of Knowledge* (New York: Vintage Books, 1998).

The cultural evolution of consciousness I had in mind, when I coined the phrase 'planetary culture' in more halcyon days, was one in which art, science, and a post-religious spirituality — like the atmosphere, continents, and ocean of a Gaian system — are never unified, but remain free and independent of one another's control, the better to embody complexity and explore the three extensive and the eight intensive dimensions of a universe made out of the music of vibrating strings.

CHAPTER 5

We Become What We Hate

Reflections on 9/11 for Planetary Culture and the Global War against Terrorism

In any passionate conflict, there is a psychological exchange of characteristics. Since the evolution of the nucleated cell that brought us sex and death for a genetically endowed indivdual, a biological foundation was laid down for the psychological relationship of Eros and Thanatos in a diploid exchange of physical traits in sex and spiritual traits in death. We slay with technology and save the victim with art. For Ice Age humans, the hibernating cave bear they stealthfully killed in the cave was saved in art, as the shaman took on its skin, and the artist appropriated its lair as its new sanctuary, and the claw scratchings on the cave wall as the numinous place to restore the animals in art.

A more recent example of this intimate process of transformation of enemy into artform can be seen in the life Richard Aitken-roshi, who went from being a Japanese prisoner of war to becoming a postwar master of Japanese Zen. After the Second World War, the entangled cultures of America and Japan moved apart in a national form of cellular mitosis, and Detroit automotive factories appeared in Japan and Zen monasteries were built in California.

In this psychological exchange of opposites, World War II was like the Crusades, for out of the attacks of Western Christendom on the Holy Land no lasting territory was gained, but the disunited Caliphates learned to reform themselves into larger imperial states, and the

62   *Self and Society*

Crusaders came home with the cultural expressions of the more advanced Islamic civilization, as Arabic music and songs, as well as their scientific and philosophical texts, enriched the European culture of the thirteenth century and laid the foundation for the Italian Renaissance and the subsequent developments of 'Western' science with da Vinci and Galileo.

A less spiritual example can be seen with the right wing extremists in modern Israel. When the victims of the Nazi holocaust returned to Zion, they showed what they had absorbed from their tormentors in the use of terror to achieve political ends in the Stern Gang bombing of the King David Hotel, and even to this day this foundational pattern survives in Sharon's government, which is the only 'civilized' nation of 'the West' in which imprisonment without trial, torture, and assasination are considered legitimate instruments of the state to protect its 'Lebensraum'. We become what we hate.

And here we are, only a year into the life of a new century and a new millennium, but at it again in another world war. But this war is not between nations or empires, or a crusade between opposed religions. It is a war between two global noetic polities — between two organizations of consciousness that seek to define human identity.

Of human systems of political identity there are basically five:

1. Sanguinal identity
2. Territorial identity
3. Linguistic identity (language and religion)
4. Economic identity (class and nation)
5. Noetic identity (scientific and spiritual)

A sanguinal identity is one that derives from descent from a common ancestor, as is evidenced in the expression, 'the children of Abraham'. Sanguinal identity is basically tribal in nature. After tribal identity came the mixtures of tribes and clans, first in city-states, and then in empires. This system of identity was based upon a territorial location and shared religious beliefs, but in the evolution of the medieval empire into the modern industrial nation-state, personal identity became based, not so much on land-tenure and religion, as economic class and national allegiance. In the twentieth century, however, the industrial nation-state became stretched out of shape and distorted from the impacts of electronic technologies of information and jet travel. In the sixties, global economists liked to point to the multinational corporation and credit it for putting national 'sovereignty at bay', but the cultural process of planetization is more complicated than that, for it also

involves the emergence of a new Complex Dynamical mathematical-artistic mentality, as well as an emotional recoil into simplistic
belief systems. The informational overload created by the new electronic technologies became shadowed by fundamentalisms, just as
jet travel became shadowed by terrorism.

We can appreciate the significance of mathematical-artistic mentalities if we look at the two shifts that preceded the emergence of the
modern 'West' with its secular industrial nation-state. In the shift
from the classical to the medieval world, there was a deep structural
shift from the Geometrical Mentality to the Algebraic Mentality, and
in this shift, Islam was as critical to its formation, as ancient Egypt
and Greece had been to the articulation of the Geometrical Mentality. Al Khawarizmi and his House of Wisdom in Bagdad both con-
solidated the mathematical developments that reached back to
Persian Jandhishapur and Chaldean Babylon and took another step
forward in the development of algebra. The Islamic interdiction
against idols and barbarian concretization actually served to energize a new sense of abstraction and appreciation of a celestial code
that expressed itself in mathematics and the new and less concrete
and more portable system of Indo-Arabic numeration in the beauty
of Arabic calligraphy, and as well in the erotic mysticism of Persian
poetry. This interconnection of an angelic dictation with the Koran, a
rising Neoplatonic mysticism, and an erotic transfiguration of individual love beyond the arranged marriages of the social order
became widespread throughout the entire Mediterranean cultural-ecology. From Layla and Majnun to Wis and Ramin to Tristan
and Isolde and Lancelot and Guinevere, and from the Sufi odes of
Ibn Arabi with his hymns to the mystical eternal feminine of Nizam
to the celestial hymn of Dante to Beatrice, a new kind of romantic
love called the soul away from the demands of the arranged marriages of the concrete social order. This Algebraic Artistic and Mathematical Mentality was a new movement of celebration of the
angelic Celestial Intelligences of a new transcendental ontology that
expressed itself in Sufism, the Zohar, and Christian mysticism. If we
take a satellite look from on high down on this cultural-ecology of
the Mediterranean at this time, there really is no such thing as 'Western Civilization'. There is Abrahamic Civilization — a basin shared
by Western, Byzantine, and Islamic streams of enrichment.

'Western Civilization' is basically an artificial construct — a cur-
ricular development that was set in place to meet the expanding
needs of the middle class as it moved into universities. Before World

War I and II, a lower school was sufficient for the working class and a 'High School' was sufficient for the clerical class. University was only needed for the professional classes of clergy, law, medicine and science. To enculturate the masses, Harvard and the University of Chicago developed their curricula of Western Civilization with its Great Books, and this was the model for the liberal arts education I received at Pomona College in California in the nineteen-fifties. 'Western Civ' was the required freshman course.

But the bifurcation that appeared to set 'the West' on its own evolutionary course did not occur with the ancient Greeks; it occurred later, around 1688. With the codification of Galilean dynamics into the calculus of movement of Newton and Leibniz, Western Europe began to surpass the hitherto advanced Ottoman Empire. With the founding of a national bank in London as a consequence of the influence of the Dutch on the Glorious Revolution of the English, the identity of a culture began to derive its value from the future instead of the past. National indebtedness allowed society to expand its investment in the infrastructure of transportation, and look to the future when one's ship came in and the investment paid off. The Ottomans looked back to the Prophet, and the Ming Chinese looked backed to their ancestors and the Mandate from Heaven, but the Dutch and the English looked to the future and to their children, and children began to show up as objects of attention in Western portraiture. Education now became important and it began to expand along with the new expanding middle classes in the new industrial nation-state in which 'sovereignty' was no longer held by the sovereign, but by the Parliament and the state. But even this progressive formation of Western Europe and North America should not be looked upon as an exclusive development of 'Western Civilization', for what supported this economic expansion with its economy of Baroque display was African slavery. Consequently, a discourse of 'Western Civilization' that does not take into its account the underclass of West African slaves and the middlemen of Arabic slave traders is literally a patriotic fiction, if not an outright lie.

The classical Geometrical Mentality had been one of fixed and unchanging values — the Chinese 'Mandate from Heaven' or the Platonic cosmos in which Eternity was the realm of ideal forms and change itself was seen as a fallen state of being. But often in history, evil becomes the annunciation of the next level of organization. So what was evil and fallen for the medieval mind became the focus of attention for the modern. The movement of money with interest created value and challenged both the medieval Papal and Islamic interdictions against usury. The movement of sailing vessels expanded the whole idea of a world, the movement of cannon balls destroyed fixed medieval fortifications, and the Copernican movement of the earth around the sun ended the perfect circles of Ptolemy's solar system, much as Harvey's new understanding of the circulation of the blood redefined ancient Roman Galenic medicine. Artistically, the rise of portraiture and the shift from poetic epic to prose novel expressed the movement of the middle classes out of their fixed places in feudal society into a new and valued story of individuation. The climactic expression of this new mentality of motion was expressed in the calculus of Leibniz and Newton.

Such was the bifurcation from medievalism to modernism, but now we are in the bifurcation from modernism to planetary culture. Since most people prefer to think of history as a collection of dates, I offer the date of 1889 as the birth of planetary culture. In 1889, Poincaré founded chaos dynamics and showed that the solar system was chaotic and not an orderly and repetitively eliptical system. 1889 also was the year in which the Universal Exhibition of Paris brought Gamalan music from Indonesia to Paris to the astonished delight of Satie, and from its complex rhythms, he reformed his whole notion of time as a simple linear sequence and succession of quantitative units. Bergson's elaboration of time as *durée* and Proust's excavation of past time with the taste of the *madeleine* came fast upon the wake of Poincaré and Satie. 1889 was also the first time in modern history that a human structure — the Eiffel Tower — became taller than the Great Pyramid. So 1889 can be settled upon as the emergence of Paris as the intellectual capital of the world — as Walter Benjamin has canonized it — and the emergence of a *noetic polity*: a distributive state of consciousness and parallel processing in science and art that was not a single ideology or simply a political or trading capital. In this bifurcation from the Galilean Dynamical to the Complex Dynamical Mentality, Western Civilization began to move out of linear systems of reductionist causation to complexity and chaos, self-organizational forms of emergence, and new appreciations of a classical Indian idea that had been presented by the Buddha and philosophically articulated by Vasubandhu and Nagarjuna, but had been overlooked by the West — the idea of 'dependent co-orgination' (*pratityasamutpadha*).

Globalization, of course, is only half the story. Around the world, leaders of nativistic movements were seeking to deny the cultural shift to a new Complex Dynamical mentality in a reactionary effort to return to the mentality that had preceded the rise of modernism and globalization. There was the Mah'di in the Sudan, the Ghost Dance in the United States, and soon to come, the Boxer Rebellion in China and the revolutions of Pearse in Ireland and Zapata in Mexico in which the apotheosis of the peasant became the new myth of revolution — a myth that would be taken up in theme and variation by Lenin, Gandhi, Mao, and Castro.

If we recall that in the thirteenth-century the Iberian fusion of Islamic, Jewish, and Christian cultures was followed by the Inquisition, and that the Protestant Reformation was followed by the Counter-Reformation and the Age of Absolutism, we will not be surprised to observe that planetization was followed by nativistic movements that sought to block the cultural transformation by returning to caricatured and highly reductionist versions of a sacred tradition. We might be surprised, however, to notice — in affirmation of Marshall McLuhan's tetrad from his *Laws of Media*[1] — that the new Complex Dynamical Mentality obsolesced the Guttenberg and Galilean mentality, but retrieved the archaic and oral mentalities that had been previously obsolesced by an imperiously expanding scientific and linear rationalist process of modernization. William James worked to retrieve the varieties of mystical experience, Freud and Jung worked to excavate an unconscious, and in the beginning of the twentieth century, shamanism and Theosophy began to be popular and highly influential for artists such as Kandinsky, Mondrian, and Kupka. In fact, the Russian anthropologist Vladimir Bogoras pointed out that when Minkowski tried to explain Einstein's relativistic time-shifts, he told parables that were similar to the relativistic time-shifts found in the folktales of Central Asian shamanism.

Globalization is an economic consolidation of *space* in world trade, but a nativistic movement is led by a prophetic figure who is experiencing a compensatory mythologizing of *time* in an interiorization of visionary consciousness. In this interiorization of time, the mystics and the scientists found themselves taking different paths up the same mountain. And this is still the case today, as the Dalai Lama invites every other year a group of scientists to his home in the foothills of the Himalayas in Dharamsala to enter into discussions with meditation practioners concerning the nature of consciousness.

---

[1]   Marshall and Eric McLuhan, *Laws of Media: the New Science* (Toronto: University of Toronto Press, 1988), p. 7.

The second wave of planetization came in 1972, when catastrophe theory was evolving into chaos dynamics, when the first paper of Lovelock's Gaia hypothesis was published, and when Denis and Donnela Meadows attempted to formulate computer models for the relationship between the global economy and the global ecology. At the same time there arose a popular interest in meditation and consciousness exploration through mystical traditions such as yoga, Sufism, Zen, and Tibetan Buddhism. Alternative institutions such as Esalen and my own Lindisfarne Association (founded in 1972) were created to bridge the anti-spirituality of the university and the anti-intellectuality of the ashram by creating a new kind of conference in which Tibetan lamas, Hopi elders, astronauts, poets, and scientists such as Bateson, Varela, Lovelock, Margulis, and Kauffman could meet in an effort to articulate and energize this new planetary culture.

But for every action there is a reaction, for every light there is a shadow. The environmental and alternative movement of the seventies was followed by President Reagan, rather than a President Jerry Brown, and Reagan worked vigorously to check its growth and reverse the environmental movement, and in this effort he has been greatly assisted by the two Presidents Bush.

Conservatives and Reactionaries have difficulty dealing with the complexity of the pattern recognition of isomorphisms in science, spirituality, and art, and prefer a simple political ideology and an emotional simplification through intensity that results in an eliminativist system of belief. Christian fundamentalists become like their enemies in atheistic modernist rationalism and inflict upon themselves a narrow and linear system of reductionism. We become what we hate

This elimination of complexity in a simplistic doctrine can be camouflaged by many different contents — not simply religious, but also political and technological — such as we saw in the twentieth century movements of Hitler and Stalin. The philosophy of science itself is not immune from this ideological process of oversimplification. In the sociobiology of E. O. Wilson, the robotics of Hans Moravec, and the eliminativist cognitive science of Patricia and Paul Churchland, we have examples of a scientistic ideology that irons out the complexity of space, time, and mind onto a flat surface that becomes the political base for the ambitions of a new scientific elite. If the sciences were all unified according to the consilient program of E. O. Wilson, a new kind of scientific Taliban would create a new scientific *Sharia* law for the technological society.

Our biosphere is a complex system in which ocean, atmosphere, and continent are different but equally contribute to the Gaian self-regulating system of the planet. An ecology of consciousness for a planetary culture would require a similar system of difference and contribution in which science, art, and spirituality are not unified in a single consilient ideology. Science left to itself can become authoritarian, as a total explanation becomes totalitarian. Religion left to itself can become equally authoritarian and violent, as we saw in the Crusades, which were first established to secure the Holy Land, were then used to militarily defend the Papacy, and were then used to eliminate heretics in the Albigensian Crusade. After the success of this genocide in France, the Inquisition was set up as a permanent institution. Art may be less horrific than religion, but that is because art has never had political power in its own right. But art left to itself can become narcisstic. In a Batesonian ecology of mind that energizes difference, it is the circularity of the triple and independently powerful descriptions of the world in science, art, and spirituality that contributes to the freedom and health of our secular society in which church and state are constitutionally bound to be separate. We would lose our freedom immediately if one domain were to win out over the other two in E. O. Wilson's program of consilience,[2] or if government were wed to faith-based social services, as these organizations would really serve to establish a civic religion and suppress secular humanism.

The new Complex Dynamical Mentality is not a political ideology, but an ecology of consciousness in which opposites are constitutive of a larger system. Like the oceans, continents, and atmosphere that are interlocked in the Gaian emergent domain, this new mathematical-artistic mentality can be embodied and energized by differing mathematicians, scientists, artists, as well as spiritual contemplatives of a more post-religious orientation — folk such as James Lovelock, Lynn Margulis, Philip Glass, Robert Bly, and the Dalai Lama.

If the Complex Dyanmical Mentality can be embodied by individuals of differing beliefs and intellectual orientations, the eliminativist mentality, by contrast, works to enforce intellectual uniformity. For the religious, political, and scientistic fanatic, not

---

[2]   E. O. Wilson, *Consilience: the Unity of Knowledge* (New York: Vintage Books, 1999).

only love and compassion, joy and suffering, but also humor, a playful sense of ambiguity, and a delight in complexity are lost in a rigidification of belief. Eliminativist cognitive science is the Kansas monocrop of consciousness: ecological diversity is eliminated in a state-wide system of sameness held in place by the machines and chemicals of agribusiness.

The Islamic fundamentalist who believes one does not have to read any book of science because the Koran was the final book is similar to this kind of cognitive scientist who believes that his is the ultimate science of consciousness and that we can ignore any philosophical notion of the Self because it is simply a piece of folk psychology and myth. For these reductionists, the mind is really nothing more than a digital information-processing machine that can be greatly improved by the association or implantation of newer and faster computers.[3] If there is no Self, then a patient in a hospital who is feeling angst or pain is simply processing phantom signals and he or she should be ignored and be treated by the scientific professionals who know better. In other words, in this scientized world, the ill and the unscientific lose their civil liberties. Agribusiness wed to the pharmaceutical industry creates medibusines, and when medibusiness is wed to edubusiness, we have the ritalin-fed, media feedlots of today's public schools.

Whatever ideological face this mental structure of simplification through emotional intensity takes on, the creature within is characterized by a revulsion to complexity and a messianic sense of self-empowerment that envisions God, or Science, or some deified historical process as giving the chosen ones a license to kill. Whether they are a Unibomber sending letter bombs to professors of computer science, or God-fearing Christians shooting doctors and blowing up abortion clinics, or Muslims blowing up passenger jets, they are souls in torment who cannot understand or accept the evolutionary transformation of civilization from one mathematical-artistic mentality to another. Planetary culture to them is a 'new world order conspiracy'.

This fundamentalist simplification through intensity amounts to an implosion of consciousness. Whether it is the case of Arabs dancing in the street in celebration of the destruction of the World Trade Center, or that of the Reverends Jerry Falwell and Pat Robertson saying on television that as ministers of the Lord they were professionals in

---

[3]   See Ray Kurzweil, *The Age of Spiritual Machines* (New York: Viking, 1999).

knowing the mind of God and knew that Jahweh was angry at Gays, liberal women, and members of the A.C.L.U., and therefore had allowed the World Trade Center to be bombed, we see a similar collapse of complexity in an expression of religious fundamentalism. For rural Christian fundamentalists, New York had always been Sin City -- the Sodom of the contemporary world, so its partial destruction made them feel relieved that God was finally taking a firm hand to the end of human history. In fact, they would rather have Armageddon than move through a cultural transformation into the new mathematical-artistic mentality of Planetization.

Fundamentalism can be Islamic, Christian, Zionist, Marxist, or Scientistic. The Zionist settler who machine gunned muslims at prayer in a mosque and became a hero to the Jewish settlers on the West Bank is brother to the terrorists who attacked New York. The danger in having a world war in which the combatants are fundamentalists is that there are bad guys on both sides, and when our bad guys lock onto their bad guys, they can eliminate everyone and everything else in the crossfire. To watch the fundamentalist Attorney General Ashcroft call for new emergency powers to override the civil liberties of a secular civil society so that the government can fight the Islamicist terrorists more effectively is also terrifying. An educated citizenry would remember Thucydides's comments on the Corcyrean Revolution, as well as the McCarthyism of the fifties, and would know better. But we ceased being an educated society when television made politics an extension of the entertainment industry.

President Bush said that we were attacked because we were a beacon of freedom. One can understand why political leaders might be feeling nervous and needing to cover their culpability with patronizingly simple rhetoric, unthinking flag-waving, and calls for patriotic support of the Commander-in-Chief, because both Republican and Democratic Presidents have made Faustian bargains with devils that have endangered us all. This is not a time to suspend civilian review of the C.I.A., or return the F.B.I. to the good old days of J. Edgar Hoover. We need to remember that it was through the C.I.A'.s overthrow of Mossadegh and our installation of the Shah that we became hated in Iran. We did this for the politics of oil, not the politics of the American Republic. Our political leaders, Democrat and Republican, chose to support the Mudjhadeen to counter the Soviet Empire; then they abandoned them and thus aided the process by which the Taliban took over Afghanistan. Our Western leaders in the U.S., France, and Germany chose to support and sell arms to Sadam Hussein to serve as a Bath Socialist counter to clerical Iran, just as now they will have to support authoritarian regimes in Pakistan and Saudi Arabia to counter Bin Laden.

And for fifty years, our political leaders have chosen not to support the original UN mandate that there should be two nations in Israel, as even now they support Sharon's policy to reduce the Palestinians to an internal proletariat in small and dispersed reservations. As a depressed proletariat, the Palestinians are expected by Sharon to serve as a pool of cheap labor for an advanced Israeli technological state. It is hard for Americans to protest, since Sharon is trying to do to the Palestinians what we did to the native Americans with our nineteenth century racist policies. But any twelve-year old with a map can see that there really can be no viable peace agreement that doesn't give the Palestinians at least Gaza, the West Bank, and East Jerusalem as an administrative center. With our never-discussed and never- debated American support for right wing Israeli efforts to put Jewish settlers in Gaza and the West Bank, we have allowed our foreign policy to become hijacked by extremists who have become the oppressive tyrants they hated in Nazi Germany. In fact, on CNN, after the discotheque suicide bombing, an Israeli teenage girl proposed a final solution to the Palestinian problem: 'They are all monsters! We should kill them all!' We become what we hate. But when the Palestinians revolt, Senator Clinton sides with Israel immediately, deplores the violence on their side, and says nothing about Sharon's policy of assasination and hyper-military counter-response with tanks and jets.

Our political leaders are rightfully nervous that we might begin to wonder why they have made us so hated by Muslims from Morocco to the Phillipines that there are more than a few martyrs willing to die in suicide attacks on the monuments of our secular globalist culture. They are nervous because they know their oil foreign policy is not that of the country as a whole or American labor in particular. After World War II, capital investments in the American oil industry were increasingly shifted abroad in an effort to avoid the costs of American labor and extraction. The virtues of this shift were not openly discussed and debated, anymore than our foreign policy is now. Instead, Bush puts his trust in the power of propoganda and the ability of the corporate ownership of the media to manipulate our emotions and keep us entranced with slogans of freedom, hanging out the flag, and singing 'God Bless America'.

But there are some Americans who might not cherish the Bush and Cheney Gulf wars and oil business deals with the Middle East that send out the children of the poor to fight and die to maintain the economic interests of the rich. There are some Americans as well as Arabs who might wish to protest the process of economic globalization in which Monsanto sues a neighboring farmer for violating its patent rights simply because his fields had been wind-swept and taken over by the pollen of Monsanto's patented alien corn. There are Americans who might not wish to see multinational corporations patent animals and plants and take over the human genome as private property — just as once the British parliament passed the Enclosure Acts that enabled the landlords to declare that the medieval commons was their private property and begin the process that forced the poor off the land and into the factories and slums of Manchester and Birmingham — which is another historical model for Sharon's policy in Palestine.

To envision this conflict of opposing noetic polities in the cultural process of planetization, I would like to go back to a model I used for 'Values and Conflict' in an essay from *At the Edge of History* that I wrote in the midst of the Viet Nam War.

Share Belief in Militarism

Liberals   Conservatives

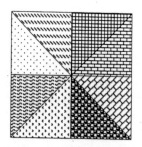

Gaian Ecumené

Global Economy

Radicals   Reactionaries

Share Belief in Revolutionary Violence

To use a pattern symbolism for the four quadrants of Liberal, Conservative, Radical, and Reactionary, we can say that the polka dot and wavy line triangles share a participation in planetary culture and desire a Gaian Ecumené; their opposites on the Right, the patterns of brick triangles of the Conservatives and Reactionaries, share participation in the industrial culture of globalization. The zigzag and thatch triangles represent the intellectuals who serve the industrialists, the globalist Harvard-style intellectuals who are attracted to power in Washington. The chevron and darkest triangles represent the Rightist Libertarians and Radical Leftists who share their distrust of Washington and Cambridge, and share a belief in revolutionary violence. The Libertarian wants his rifle to fight the world-order conspiracy, and the radical Leftist seeks to turn peaceful anti-globalists demonstrations into riots by throwing Molotov cocktails at department stores and globalist businesses. The polka dot and the wavy line triangles represent the environmentalists and intellectuals outside the established Harvard-MIT-Washington establishment. The zigzag and thatch triangles represent the Establishment and share a commitment and participation in the electronic technologies and believe in the necessary application of technological force to advance state aims, whereas the radicals and reactionaries share a commitment to nativistic and visionary beliefs and seek a return to 'nature' or pre-industrial cultures, but also share a belief in force to advance revolutionary aims. Violence on the part of the state is called military operations; violence on the part of the revolutionaries or the stateless is called terrorism by those holding the monopoly on state violence. In the form of nativistic terrorism, these acts can be ecoterrorist destruction of stripmining equipment, animal rights bombings of laboratories, Christian fundamentalist bombings of abortion clinics or murders of doctors, and, of course, Islamicist hijackings, suicide bombings, and anthrax attacks. My sympathies are obviously in the Gaian triangles, and so I am sympathetic to science, work with computers and the Internet, prefer a post-religious contemplatively spiritual way of life, and wish to see an environmental movement of ecological designs and 'living machines' in which bacterial cultures are used to digest and render non-toxic the by-products of scientific and technological activities.[4] In my Gaian utopian fantasy, the whales have evolved brains for

---

[4]   See Nancy Jack Todd and John Todd, *From Eco-Cities to Living Machines: Principles of Ecological Design* (North Atlantic Books: Berkeley, CA, 1994).

composing great Brahmsian symphonies in the seas and are capable of beaming them to the stars and listening to their answer in the music of the spheres. For me, the sonic shattering of the whales brains through the sonar blasts of our atomic submarines is an unfathomable evil.

This archetypal fourfold model enables us to see that sometimes individuals in opposite parties are much closer than they are to some members within their own party. A Leftist Green may be closer to a Rightist Libertarian than to a Clinton or Gore Liberal.

With good and evil distributed on both sides of our global conflict, what we are dealing with in our twenty-first century world is not the old battle of twentieth century ideologies — fascism, communism, and capitalism — but an ecology of consciousness in a state of per- turbation and noise. Through this increase of noise, civilization is being drawn toward a new attractor, but we cannot tell yet if this will be a periodic attractor — one oscillating between civilization and barbarism — or a complex dynamical, chaotic attractor — much like the one in which a turbulent atmosphere and a tectonically unstable system of continents and an envelopement of oceans establishes itself as a planetary Gaian system in which life can evolve. Can civili- zations co-exist in a cultural version of a Gaian system, or are we headed for a new dark age in Huntington's 'Clash of Civilizations'?

Some columnists and OpEd essayists in the *New York Times* have tried to characterize the terrorist attack on America, as an attack on 'Judeo-Christian Civilization', but such an imaginary fortress is a fictional construct that distorts the history in which Catholic crusad- ers sacked Byzantium, in which Jews were villified and slaughtered as the murderers of Christ, and in which Islam was the civilizational force that helped lift Western Europe out of barbarism and contrib- uted to the development of science beyond the Hellenistic, Persian, and Indian achievements it had inherited.[5] A better name for the cul- tural-ecology that surrounded the Mediterranean basin would be Abrahamic Civilization, since it really based itself not so much on Greek philosophy and Roman law as upon the Abrahamic religions.

Since the origins of civilization in the fourth millennium BCE, human culture has been characterized by a periodic attractor that swung back and forth between the two states of civilization and nomadic barbarism. Cities would rise, and then they would be over-

---

[5]   See Howard R. Turner, *Science in Medieval Islam* (Austin, TX: University of Texas Press, 1995).

run and sacked by Amorites, Kassites, Huns, Mongols, Goths, or Mesoamerican Chichimecs. But for the last 500 years, we appear to have shifted from this periodic attractor, oscillating between two states, to a chaotic attractor in which a polycentric and complex dynamical system of global civilization is not brought down by the wars within it. All that may be about to change if we enter upon a global war of modernism versus medievalism, a conflict in which global terrorists with no fixed location and multinational managers with no fixed address or deep intellectual culture serve as the new nomads fighting a tribal war in which the traditional civilizations are caught in the crossfire. The world knows that there is an Islam that is not that of the terrorists, but does the world know there is an America other than Hollywood, McDonalds and Coca-Cola ads that camouflage a foreign policy of arm sales and military support of authoritarian regimes?

To avoid this polarization to extremes in which the new nomads use weapons of mass destruction, we have to understand that humanity is evolving out of nation-states into a new global ecology of noetic polities, and that this new structure of consciousness is a distributive system that is not contained in a modern industrial nation-state or a medieval religion. Religion was the spiritual expression of humanity from the origins of civilization to 1945. Then, in the condition of that global break, new visions of a postreligious spirituality began to be articulated by writers such as Albert Einstein, Teilhard de Chardin, Jean Gebser, Owen Barfield, and Sri Aurobindo. In many ways, Einstein is the archetypal figure of this shift from traditional Judaism to a scientific mysticism in which the unique individual is in communion with the universe without the institutional mediation of temple or church.

Naturally, or should I say culturally, when a new structure of con-sciousness appears, the old formation does not disappear. Jean Gebser noticed that when a new human structure of consciousness appeared in history, the old structure became a *deficient* mode as the new structure became the *efficient* mode of cultural evolution.[6] When agriculture created settled communities, the shamanism of hunting and gathering societies began to decay into the deficient mode of sorcery. One can see this conflict between religion and sorcery in the Mexican myths of Quetzalcoatl versus the dark sorcerer

---

[6] Jean Gebser, *Everpresent Origin*, trans. Noel Barstad and Algis Mickunas (Athens, OH, Ohio University Press, 1985), p. 3.

Tezcatlipoca. When agricultural villages grew into urban civilizations, the charismatic magic of a prophetic figure was replaced by
the priestcraft and astronomical science of a temple institution.
Magic became the *deficient* mode, as the Mythic structure of consciousness became the leading *efficient* mode. When the modern
world shifted into the Mental structure of consciousness, the Mythical mode became the *deficient* in the Inquistion, the witch trials, and
the seventeenth-century wars of religion. The *efficient* mode of the
evolution of consciousness shifted to science and art in the new
achievements of da Vinci and Galileo. Now we are experiencing the
evolution of consciousness from the Mental to the Integral, so the
mental mode has become the deficient form in scientistic movements of technological reductionism and dehomination, and in
imperial projects of an expansive capitalistic globalization. But the
end of modernism has also brought us back to the wars of religion
with which the modern age began in the Thirty Years War — which
was really a hundred years war for the Dutch and the Irish. Religion
is not going to disappear any time soon for the multitude, but the
multitude did not create the Renaissance, nor will the multitude create the planetary renaissance. But as the religious multitudes
become more violent — with Hindus destroying mosques in India,
and Muslims attacking America, and white racists burning down
Black churches in the American South, and Skinheads destroying
Jewish cemetaries in Germany and New Jersey, and Jews machine
gunning Muslims at prayer in Palestine, the manifestations of the
deficient structure of consciousness in religion will energize the
growth of the *efficient* Integral structure of consciousness in the new
Complex Dynamical mentality in which science, art, and contemplative spirituality take us forward and not backward into the anaerobic depths of Milton's 'dark backward and abysm of time'.

What Jean Gebser did not notice, however, is that each shift in the
structure of consciousness was followed by a dark age:

1. Archaic	1. Mesolithic Dark Age, 9500 BCE
2. Magical	2. Kurgan Invasions 4500 BCE
3. Mythical	3. Aegean Dark Age, 1400 BCE
4. Mental	4. European Dark Age, 476-800 CE
5. Integral	5. Contemporary Dark Age ?

If we are not careful, this global war on terrorism could spin out of control, with weapons of mass destruction being used on both sides, so it is worth the effort to look at the big picture and see the emergence of a new structure of consciousness as an opportunity to articulate a new planetary culture that is not simply the triumphalism of the West.

In this new Integral structure of consciousness, the linear ideologies of fanatical religions and political movemensts such as fascism, communism, and imperial variants of capitalism, are inadequate expressions of the complexity in which light can be both a particle and a wave. Or in the words of Niels Bohr: 'The opposite of a fact is a falsehood, but the opposite of one profound truth may well be another profound truth'. The archetypal figure of this new postreligious spirituality for our time is the Dalai Lama, who has taken his loss of a territorial identity and reconstructed it in the form of a global teacher working to take traditional religion and traditional Western science up to a new level of global spiritual understanding. Since the seventies, I have called this formation Planetary Culture,[7] and by this I do not mean a national or ethnic culture that becomes triumphant, but a new emergent domain that is bounded and energized by the membrane of the Earth's biosphere and is characterized by new expressions of art and science that are not restricted to historically defined ideologies or groups. The ethnicities within become like the organelles within a cell. Like mitochondria, they can keep some of their ancient DNA and their intracellular unity, but their expressions now serve to energize the metabolic processes of the larger planetary cell.

Art is a better model for this process than politics, and African-American jazz is a good example of how art can serve in the transformation of identity. The presence of Africans in the United States did not develop into a separatist state within our territory, or their return to Africa — though Elijah Muhammed wanted the former, and Abraham Lincoln wanted the latter. Their presence resulted in a transformation of American identity, and what it meant 'to be American'. It no longer meant simply being white, rural, and protestant. We are now being called upon to extend that identity to Arabs in particular and Muslims in general, and America is indeed capable of effecting this shift to a multicultural civilization, although this is

[7] See William Irwin Thompson, *Passages About Earth: an Exploration of the New Planetary Culture* (New York: Harper & Row, 1974).

going to be difficult. It will require 'us' accepting 'them' in many different and mutually interactive ways. Protestant America has only recently overcome the open anti-Semitism that was common in the 1940s, and it was just beginning to accept Blacks as possible leaders and public figures, and was making some progress in the process of accepting Mexicans and other Latinos as workers among us rather than 'illegal aliens'. Now it is going to have to see Muslims as American as pita bread and apple pie. But Muslims also will need to appreciate that America is not simply an economic space in which to open a business, nor is it a culture coming out of the great age of medieval religions. The U.S. Constitution is an expression of the European philosophical Enlightenment and the secularist idea of the separation of church and state, and this movement is most definitely one that did not pass through Islamic civilization — even though Islam had its own non-secular means of protecting religious tolerance — as was seen in the great era of twelfth and thirteenth-century Spain with the cultural florescence of Ibn Arabi, Maimonodes, and Rabbi Moses de Leon. Sharia law, feminism, and the U.S. constitution are not going to be easily reconciled in some superficial version of cultural relativism or pronouncement of politically correct shibboleths.

Planetization is a cultural transformation that is composed of a shift to complex dynamical systems and a cultural retrieval of the maps of consciousness that had been effaced in the flat and linear project of global economic modernization. Yoga, Zen, Tibetan Buddhism, Sufism, Taoism, Cabbalistic mysticism, and native American shamanism all have something to teach us in this shift from the industrial nation-state to the planetary ecology of noetic polities. The contemporary practioners of these contemplative arts are not reactionaries, but often professionals working with computers and communicating through the Internet and the world wide web. But since the cultural process of planetization is intimately linked to science and technology through jet travel and electronic technologies, there is also a shadow-side to planetization that is conventionally known as globalization.

The Greens who oppose multinational corporations' use of child labor sweat shops in poor countries, or their efforts to patent genes, own the human genome, stripmine landscapes, pollute rivers and seas, overprescribe psychotropic drugs for schoolchildren, or market Frankenstein foods are also part of this cultural process of change. Capitalism, by itself, is not the enemy, for there are really two major historical forms of capitalism, the modernist variety that emerged with Galilean linear dynamics and tends to organize itself in linear and imperial systems of center (or power) and periphery (or resources) in a reductionism to domains of rich and poor; and a new form of capitalism informed by the shift to complex dynamical systems that sees the world in a phase-change from a world economy to a planetary ecumené. In the former, info-serfs labor in 'work for hire' arrangements on the plantation of Novartis or Monsanto, and all scientific inventions are owned by the corporation. In the contemporary form of capitalism that is seeking to emerge on the other side of our antimodernist rejection of capitalism, the scientists, artists, and workers participate in a mutual system of 'dependant co-origination' and mutual wealth generation. So part of the appreciation of complexity is to understand that there are good guys and bad guys on all sides in this global conflict of noetic polities, and that sometimes, as we saw in the cases of Bill Clinton or Al Gore, even inside one person. One cannot simply put one's faith into one simple institution: political, financial, religious, or academic, and trust that its leaders will be right.

President Bush should have reached out to President Khatami and the intellectuals and liberals seeking to end the tyranny of the medievalist mullahs, as this move would have helped to sublimate Iran's actions from support for Hezbollah to leadership within the new Islamic civilization and the United Nations. But Bush in his 'axis of evil' State of the Union address wanted to create new post-Cold War enemies in order to support his campaign to build an anti-missile defense program for the businessmen who put him in office to advance their interests. So when South Korea reached out in a spirit of peace to North Korea, or when President Katami reached out to the United Nations, it did not serve the economic interests of the invisible directorate of Amerika Inc. that tells the President what to say and do.

Unfortunately, we have now arrived at a situation in which an invisible and internal government inside nations such as Pakistan and Iran — as well as in 'terrorist' nations such as Iraq — can camouflage itself with Islamicist ideology, just as an internal and invisible government inside our televized American government can camouflage itself with a liberal democratic ideology of free elections — elections that are totally controlled by the process of fund-raising from the very people who own the media and constitute the invisible directorate. Like cattle, the info-serfs are fed with technoswill in media feedlots that prepare their minds for slaughter. As our internal shadow government puts away civil liberties for safekeeping in its state of permanent war against terrorists, global and domestic, it creates a situation that is ideally suited to keep itself in power indefinitely. In the days of the 'Communist Menace' of the Cold War and the McCarthy era, there was never so open and violent a domestic attack as we experienced on '9/11'. On that bright blue and sunny morning of September, I was not in Manhattan, but was in Southampton, New York, watching on TV in real time the images of the buildings collapsing that would be replayed over and over—to the terror of little children who thought that the attacks were continuing. With the general population terrorized by the images on television, the radical right now can hope to use patriotism to maintain its lock on democracy for some time to come. The very industrialists who move their American headquarters to Bermuda to avoid taxes, and move their factories outside the country to weaken American labor unions, are the very same Republican businessmen and women who will now wrap the stars and stripes around their piracies to sing 'God Bless America' on Fox News.

If we are lucky and come out of this global conflict without attacks with weapons of mass destruction on either side, we may be able to avoid the slide down into a dark age; then the positive exchange of characteristics in this conflict of noetic polities could be one in which the Islamicist camouflage falls off these anti-globalization Ché Guevara type revolutionaries, and Islam becomes part of American national consciousness, as well as part of the new twenty-first century contemporary civilization. The Islamicist revolutionaries will probably split along the old Weberian lines of routine and charisma, and the messianic will go off like Ché to die for futile anti-modernist projects, but the others like Castro — who dons a $2000 Brioni suit to meet the Pope or address the U.N. — will run the business and establish relations with viable Islamic nations. Americans, for our part, will need to help this process along by appropriating the revolutionaries' agenda through recognizing and securing the state of Palestine, withdrawing our military bases from Saudi Arabia, and looking to the United Nations to secure the process of nation-building in places like Afghanistan or Somalia.

To energize a truly more democratic and ecological vision of global civilization composed of distinct cultural biomes — one that President Khatami articulated in his address to the United Nations — the United States should have moved to affirm Iran and China's claims to be ancient and continuous civilizations that have a contribution to make to global culture. If we had openly admitted our past CIA mistakes with the overthrow of Mossadegh and our installation of the Shah, and initiated a process of working in concert with other cultures, we could begin to export an American culture that is intellectually deeper and more complex than the consumerism of Nike, Coca-Cola, McDonalds, and Rambo movies; we might then begin to be respected as a true force for the democratic ideal, and not simply a democratically camouflaged plutocracy with its own private Cheney and Rumsfeld foreign policy and an economy dependant on global arms sales to authoritarian and repressive regimes.

'*Tout comprendre est tout pardoner*' may be too much to ask of the average citizen in our global village, but compassion and a cooling down of the habit of demonizing one's opponents in politics is a good place to start. Perhaps one of the reasons that the Dalai Lama has become such a global super star is that a healthy dose of Buddhist compassion is precisely what humanity needs right now to get through this difficult era of planetary transformation in which the children of Abraham are at one another's throats.

The Myth of
American Democracy

Reflections on the Invasion of Iraq

It would now appear that the United States experienced a well-planned putsch in the election of 2000, and that both the intrusive actions of the Supreme Court, the dirty tricks tactics of the Republicans in Florida, as well as the Iraq policy of the Defense Policy Board (Woolsley, Pearle, and Wolfowitz) were all worked out in advance. The Haliburton oil dealings of Cheney seem to have successfully sidelined France and Russia's oil business interests in Saddam's Iraq, and in the American takeover, Cheney and Rumsfeld now can hope to control the second largest oil reserves on the planet, and thus challenge the oil industry of Russia and position themselves to control the economic growth of China and block the efforts of Europe to become an independent superpower. With a weak dollar and a strong Euro, American junk food, GM crops, and drugs are now cheaper than the real European thing, so it makes it harder for Europe to resist the transformation of farming from a way of life into an extraction industry. For an oil man like Bush, agribusiness is more like mining than farming, so Europe's efforts to keep out American genetically engineered products and antibiotic-infested and hormone-pumped meat just makes no sense to him or ADM, and the weak deficit-freighted dollar that the war has brought forth has the peacetime dividend of serving to price elitist Europe out of the market.

That Bush should come to power through the manipulations of the State of Florida and the Electoral College brings out into the open the inherently anti-democratic nature of American government. A candidate with a plurality of 100,000 popular votes can still lose the election because the designers of the American constitution always feared popular democracy. More than anything, rural white Southern Protestant landlords and slave owners feared the great cities of the North, such as Philadelphia, New York, and Boston, for the cities teemed with Catholics and Jews and Central Europeans. Were these masses to aggregate in the popular vote, polite society would come to an end. So elections were to be controlled by Electors in state legislatures in order that the rural states of the South could thus check the power of the urban masses of the North. Not even the American Civil War was able to eliminate this inherently anti-democratic institution, because the industrial elite soon recognized that the Electoral College could also be useful to them in locking in a plutocratic society and holding in check the power of the great unwashed in the working classes. Thus the election of little Bush revealed the great fault in American society and served to put an end to the myth of American democracy. And it did not take Bush long before he secured the rule of the many by the few with the Patriot Act, which suspended *habeas corpus* and initiated a new domestic police process in which civil liberties and the protection of dissent were profoundly weakened.

In the British parliamentary system, Gore would have become the leader of Her Majesty's opposition, but whether through complicity or stupidity, Gore caved in, abandoned the leadership of his party, went off to sulk, and experiment with new identities in a personal makeover in which he grew a beard and tried to look like a college professor. The Democratic party collapsed, and Bush was given a free hand to advance the neoconservative agenda without any philosophical discussions of its ideas.

Instinctively, the chaps in Whitehall and MI6 recognized this Old Boys Club move in the play of 'the Great Game', and could see their own historical traditions shining through the Skull and Bones society of Bush's Yale and Rumsfeld's Princeton, and so Tony Blair was told to abandon Europe, his own party and constituents, and join in with the American plan to take over Iraq. Small wonder that Robin Cook resigned. But here we need to remember that it was Britain that created this geopolitic of oil in the first place. When Churchill shifted the British navy from heavy, slow, coal-fired ships to lighter and faster oil-fired ones, he shifted Britain away from dependency on its own domestic coal reserves to a natural resource that was in the Middle East. Depending on domestic natural resources only tends to make the labour unions of the working classes uppity and a nuisance to the members of the board, so both Britain and the U.S. began to shift their investments away from domestic extraction to Middle Eastern sources where one could make a a gentleman's deal with a Sheikh or Sultan, who would then tell his medieval vassals to behave. As the allies dismembered the Ottoman Empire, new lands were drawn in the sand and fictitious units like Iraq were created so that no true nation could challenge BP and claim the right to own 'its own resources'. Britain tried to grab it all, but after the Second World War, the American companies moved in, and Persia was turned into Iran. When Mossadegh tried to nationalize the oil resources of Iran, he was overthrown by the CIA and the Shah was installed as a co-operating dictator.

Although France and Germany objected vigorously in the Security Council before the Iraq invasion, they were being duplicitous, since France always sought to have Iraq as its special oil friend, and both France and Germany had sold all the nasty stuff to Saddam Hussein that he used to build up his unAmerican version of a secret police state. Now nothing but the ungovernable anarchy of Iraq and Afghanistan seems to stand in the way of the Bush administration's reversal of the Age of Democratic Revolutions.

In a way, this Republican administration is more open and in your face about what its agenda really is than previous Democratic administrations, and so one can only marvel at how consistently the Republicans can push their agenda, and still get away with what amounts to a period of reaction not seen since Metternich's Europe. But here we need to remember that that reactionary effort to reverse history served to ignite the July Revolution in France and the general European revolutions of 1848. France and Germany would slide back into the centralized authoritarian regimes that would lead them on to the Franco-Prussian War and World War One, but Switzerland — where I am writing these reflections in the spring of 2003 — became the shining example of success for the revolutionary period of 1848 and went on to establish a middle class democratic nation-state that was balanced by a decentralized cantonal system of multi-lingual cultures and religions. The United States was never able to achieve such a direct democracy and the American Civil War only served to make the American President into an imperial Bismarck for an industrial nation-state that was terrified of its own masses of former slaves, immigrants, and unpropertied citizens. The new Patriot Act expresses this fear of the bottom by the top and has given the U.S. Government unheard of police powers that even the McCarthy era of the House on UnAmerican Activities did not have. Since dissent is being marked as unpatriotic, there is an opening now for a reactionary tsunami of legislation to eliminate environmental protection, workers' protection for safety in manufacturing, and Medicare and Medicaid. Childcare benefits to single mothers are eliminated in the same legislation that eliminates dividend taxes for investors and offers yet another tax cut to the top two percent of the country's wealthy class.

The Bush Administration has installed a military colony in Iraq to be financed with Iraq's own oil so as to create a wedge in the Islamic crescent of the Muslim world from Morocco to the Philippines. In response to 9/11, the U.S. has responded to Islamicist attack by taking on this new enemy in the way that it took on fascism in the forties and communism in the fifties. The neoconservative globalist thinkers appear to have succeeded in making the enforced modernization of Islam the Bush administration's new world project. In postwar Iraq — as it did before in postwar Germany and Japan — the United States will try to globalize laggard cultures. Turkey, tired of being rebuffed by Giscard d'Estaing, and still waiting for the European Union to let it join the club, tried to shift its interests away from what Rumsfeld calls 'Old Europe' (meaning intellectual Europe) to the U.S., and its administrative leaders tried but failed to talk its Parliament into giving permission for the stationing of American troops on the border of northern Iraq to continue the process of the secularization of the Middle East begun by Ataturk and continued by the Bath socialists. Now Turkey is out, and the Kurds are in as they are more able to govern their turf than is southern Iraq, with its civil war of secularists and Shi'ites.

With Ataturk's Turkey and a Bath socialist secular Iraq behind it in historical time, the American Defense Policy Board thought it could mount a new challenge to Islamic fundamentalism and intimidate Iran and Hezbolah in Lebanon without the need to request bases in Kuwait, or Wahabi-mad Saudi Arabia, or fly-over rights from unstable Pakistan. Jordan is already poised to follow the West; and with American troops at its border, Syria will have no choice but to fall in line, and soon even Lebanon will return to its old ways as the banking capital of the Middle East: or so would appear to be the new American imperial globalist thinking.

Think tank models have a way of losing touch with the ethnological reality of cultures on the ground, and one only need recall the political scientist's approach to modernizing Viet Nam in the sixties to suspect that these Defense Policy Board cultural theorists have no understanding of culture. It is all well and good to invoke MacArthur's postwar Japan or Germany's postwar 'Wirtschaftswunden', but Japan and Germany had deep and long-standing cultures to fall back on in a crisis of national reconstruction. The Emperor of Japan himself came on the radio to tell his people not to fight but surrender and rebuild, and the traditions of obeisance to cultural norms were so deep in Japan that it would be unthinkable to imagine the Japanese plundering their own national treasures at a time of regime collapse. Although the Americans were warned that anarchy would insue in the wake of the collapse of Saddam's police state, no one was really listening in Washington. Texan and Wyoming cowboys like Bush and Cheney don't care about culture because culture is for sissies, artists, and poets — the kind of people the ladies can have over for tea to talk about what kind of art they should buy to re-do the house — while the real men are on the other side of the house, playing poker, and talking about money and power.

Bush and Cheney revealed themselves as the Yahoos they are when they ordered the tanks to surround the oil ministry and defend it from looters — this to protect the records Haliburton needed — and said nothing about the museums, libraries, universities, and hospitals, all of which were destroyed by 'Iraquis' because they were not really Iraquis, for there is no such thing as 'the Iraqui people'. It was and still is a Western imperial fabrication.

It would have been far better if the United States had begun this process of secularization of the Middle East with the extreme Right of Greater Israel, worked to establish a viable Palestinian state, and encouraged the process of liberalization in Iran — instead of branding Iranians as partners in the Axis of Evil. But helping Liberals is not something the Bush administration likes to do. But to be fair to the Republicans, one needs to recognize that American foreign policy is based on industrial interests and not simply on party politics. America prefers dictators to liberals because dictators buy up our old military inventory, and thus finance our military modernizations through which we keep ahead of the pack. After all, it was a Democratic FDR who uttered the immortal lines about the Latin American dictator Somoza, 'He may be a son-of-a-bitch, but he is our son-of-a-bitch'. And it was a Democratic Harry Truman who served American industrial interests to create the National Security State with its founding of the Central Intelligence Agency in 1947. America has always needed an enemy to define itself. After the War of Independence, we demonized the savages to get their land, and continued our imperial expansion with one war after another, from 1812 to the Mexican War and the Spanish American War and on to all the wars of the twentieth century.

If one considers the historical example of the greatness of the Dutch in using commerce and war to establish the new capitalism in their era of brilliance in the seventeenth century, then one can recognize that war and capitalism have been co-dependant since the birth of the modern nation-state. Therefore, we cannot look to a Democratic Administration to save us from the excesses of a Republican one. In many ways, little Bush is literally a godsend, for in his theme park patriotic rhetoric and his phoney body language, he reveals himself clearly to be a liar, but that sort of pathological liar who succeeds as a con-man because he can suspend disbelief in an act of poetic faith in believing his own fictions. Democratic Presidents like FDR, Truman, and Clinton were more dangerous in that they were more successful in convincing their electorates that they were really democrats at heart and that America was basically a democratic and not a plutocratic society.

But this new century's batch of Republicans does seem to have raised deception to a new level. In his political platform of 'compassionate conservatism', Karl Rove unblinkingly announced a Republican program that was the opposite of what they all secretly intended. When Bush spoke about reforming education, he really meant dumbing the population down even further with corporate ownership of the media, for the last thing the Republicans want is an educated and critically empowered free society. When Bush spoke of 'faith-based charities', he meant the destruction of the social welfare system. When he spoke of giving the small investor in social security a better return on his money, he meant dismantling the social safety net set in place by FDR after the Depression. When he spoke of Defense, he meant a new system of offensive projections aimed at preventing any state from moving to military parity with the U.S. When he spoke of freedom, he meant a new system of Patriot Act laws that would dismantle civil liberties and eliminate dissent. When he spoke of patriotism, he meant rewarding his golf partners for moving their corporate headquarters out of the U.S. to tax havens in Bermuda and their factories outside the country to Mexico, Indonesia, or China. And when Bush spoke about stimulating the economy through tax cuts, he meant ruining the nation-state economy, weakening the dollar by running up huge deficits so as to drive the Euro through the roof and cheapen the cost of American arms, genetically manipulated crops, drugs, and heavy equipment so as to reorder the world along the new industrial lines that have nothing to do with the lives of middle class citizens in nation-states, European or American.

Neither Republican nor Democratic administrations have ever liked good guys, because good guys build hospitals and schools for their societies, and American business doesn't make any money from that. Perhaps if we started building exportable health systems — starting with a good one for ourselves — ecological systems for environmental remediation, and educational software in place of military hardware, we might find other means of making money from our exports, and would not need an expensive anti-missile shield against the enemies we keep energizing with our pernicious ways. Saddam Hussein and the Taliban, in truly Orwellian fashion, used to be last month's friends against last month's enemies, and we need to remember that if terrorists have Stinger missiles it is because Brzezinski, the National Security Adviser, gave them to the Taliban in Afghanistan to fight the Soviets. Now last month's allies are this month's enemies, and in response to this primitive American habit of always needing an enemy to define itself and support its economy, al Qaeda will be happy to play its part as the global enemy of globalization and continue to try to violate the hitherto remote and invulnerable territorial integrity of the United States.

With invisible enemies everywhere, and with a terrorized population patriotically following the leader, the never-ending war against terrorism will be good for the Bush administration's hypercapitalist hostile takeover of the middle class nation-state. Capitalism is a system of doing business with and for investors, clients, and customers, but hypercapitalism is a system of using the manipulation of the stock price, and the confiscation of pension funds, to play a game in which the executives ignore the investors, employees, and customers to pay themselves millions as they bail out in their golden parachuttes and head on to other acts of piracy. Hypercapitalism is the new business world of Enron, World Com, Arthur Anderson, and Swissair. Cheney Rumsfeld Bush and Company are now free to dupe the investors, raid the pension funds by recylcing Social Security's trillions of dollars through friends' hands in investment banks, eliminate dividend taxes — at the same time that it destroys public health by building down Medicare, Medicaid, and environmental defenses in order to build up an antimissile defense system that is good for Raytheon and partners. Just as Enron raided the corporation to bilk the investors, employees, clients, and customers — from the little guy to the giant State of California — so now do Bush's off-camera producers seek to strip the assets of the nation-state to create a small invisible directorate that can control all the jet fuel and gas at the pump for the masses on the planet and thus control the competing development of Europe, Russia, and China. In the enantiodromias of history, it is now Amerika über Alles! — or, to be more precise, the board of directors of Amerika Inc.

9/11 proved that an enemy does not need an intercontinental missile to reach our shores, and also proved to President Bush's handlers that a domestic terrorist attack is the most effective way to sustain a flawed leader's popularity. So if al Qaeda doesn't provide them with another timely attack, the producers can manufacture one of their own. After all, if you can take over the Supreme Court, and the media, reality can be arranged by outsourcing a nasty contract to deeply camouflaged Special Ops, much in the way that the Kennedys once sought Mafia help in the elimination of Castro.

To expect that the U. S. government can effect a paradigm shift to create a new economy that is not based upon an enemy is, of course, naïve, but SARS has shown us that public health is truly our first line of defense, so liberals may know something that the conservatives have forgotten. Even global business depends upon global public health. But with the media under the control of a few individuals like Murdock and Malone, the American people will believe whatever they see and are told to believe on Fox, CNN, and WNBC. Since the FCC has structured the communications media so that candidates cannot use them for populist Town Hall style meetings during what should be intensely shortened elections, political life is now a media Superbowl of the permanent Presidential campaign. Ads are paid by campaign fund-raising with the very media corporations that get their money back from the sale of campaign advertizing on their airwaves. Since Democrats also have to raise money from these same media corporation moguls to pay for their own campaign commercials, they are not able to offer a truly democratic alternative and will go along with this permanent lockout of democracy and put forward candidates like Senators Lieberman and Clinton who think in the same well-worn ruts of mass media culture. With a dumbed-down population held in thrall by reality TV and fake news, American democracy is caught like a mammoth in the La Brea tarpits.

When Harry Truman created a National Security State, he did so at the same time that he expanded the middle class through the G. I. Bill that built the suburbs and sent a generation of young men to college. Republicans may talk about the free market system, and resisting government intervention in the private sector, but they all got rich because of massive postwar government intervention into the private sector. The National Defense Act paid for the interstate highway system, which gave us freeways and shopping malls next to the subdivision tracts paid for by the G.I. Bill; and the Cold War gave us the enemy we needed to keep our aerospace industries going in 'peace time'. Republicans really know this at heart, and that is why — though they talk of small government — they spend a lot of their time at fund raisers to produce the funds to keep government under their control.

The social experiment of the Bush conservatives seems intent on pushing the middle class back into the working class where it is forced to compete for survival with a new immigrant class and cheaper labor from factories moved abroad beyond environmental and union constraints: in other words, back to the state of America around 1900, before the waves of social legislation of the twentieth century. But intellectually degraded Americans may prove to be much easier to rule than the rest of the world — as recent world-wide demonstrations indicate. Not surprisingly, this cowboy strategy is better at bombing than building nation-states, and as long as Somalia, Afghanistan, Iraq, and Palestine remain ungovernable, it will be harder for the conservatives to carry on with this old paradigm economy of more foreign attacks and more domestic deficits. But they will soldier on, and, indeed, they now seek to uncork the nuclear genie to develop and use tactical nuclear weapons in order to take on North Korea. But if Bush uses tactical nukes to take out Kim Il's bunker in North Korea, or Osama Bin Laden's escarpment in Eastern Pakistan, al Qaeda will probably move back inside Saudi Arabia and organize a revolution to bring down the monarchy and replace it with the same crazy Wahabiism the Saudi family tolerated to support itself by diverting attention away from it to the infidels.

A cascade of events that can disintegrate the world-system has probably already been released and all the players in the world-system are now beginning to move independently of the old system of collective restraints. It is noise that draws a system toward a new attractor, and the noise of nation-states is dissolving this old post-World War II international system of the P5 of the Security Council. The American invasion of Iraq has created a new attractor in which China — now distracted with SARS — can feel authorized to move on Taiwan. North Korea and al Qaeda now have nothing to lose in becoming the spoilers of the world game of global capitalism. Spoilers do not need to balance strategy with compromise and can simply choose to seek an Islamic resacralization of a broken world by initiating a world depression through anthraxing Wall Street and taking out electronic capitals with black market nukes. In the words of the old Chinese curse — 'May you live in interesting times!' — we do seem to be cursed to be living in more than interesting times.

We could indeed slide into a global depression followed by mass starvations of over-populated societies now dependant on artificial agricultural life support, and this, in turn, could cascade into a dark age that could last a century. Remember that after the brief florescence of middle class capitalism and art in Renaissance Italy, Europe developed a new aristocratic world economy that was supported by global slavery and held in place through religious inquisitions and war. In the Age of Absolutism, the Age of Democratic Revolutions had to wait until the eighteenth century for the Enlightenment to pick up the stalled project of the Renaissance to continue with the development of the rights of the individual. So as we watch the myth of American democracy die before our eyes, we can think of Rome and reread our Gibbon, or remember the French and German generals of World War One who leapt into war with enthusiasm and great abandon in 1914. Like those stupid generals who lifted the banners of patriotism to prepare a generation for slaughter, our national leaders seem to be playing the old world game of waging millions of human lives for the sake of protecting the delusions of the few in Israel and the United States.

Bibliography

Abraham, Ralph (in press), 'The geometry of angels' in *Bolts from the Blue: Mathematics and Cultural Evolution* (Rhinebeck, NY: Monkfish Books).

Anderson, William (1983), *Dante the Maker* (London: Hutchinson).

Ascher, Marcia (2002), *Mathematics Elsewhere: an Exploration of Ideas Across Cultures* (Ithaca, NY: Princeton University Press.

Barnstone, Willis (1984), *The Other Bible: Jewish Pseudepigrapha, Christian Apocrypha, Gnostic Scriptures, Kabbalah, and Dead Sea Scrolls* (San Francisco, CA: Harper Collins).

Benjamin, Walter (1974), 'Paris,die Hauptstadt des XIX Jahrhunderts' in *Illuminationen: Ausgewaehlte Schriften* (Frankfurt am Main: Suhrkamp).

Braudel, Fernand (1984), *Civilization and Capitalism, Fifteenth–Eighteenth Century, Volume III, The Perspective of the World* (London: Fontana, Harper Collins).

Cheour, M. *et al.* (2002), 'Psychobiology: Speech sounds learned by sleeping newborns', *Nature*, 415, pp. 599–600.

Dehaene, Stanislas (1997), *The Number Sense: How the Mind Creates Mathematics* (London, Penguin).

Dodd, E.R. (1951), 'From shame-culture to guilt-culture', in *The Greeks and the Irrational* (Berkeley, CA: University of California Press).

Donald, Merlin (2001), *A Mind So Rare: The Evolution of Human Consciousness* (New York: Norton).

Farmer, Steve (1998), *Syncretism in the West: Pico's 900 Theses (1486): The Evolution of Traditional Religious and Philosophical Systems* (Tempe, AZ: Medieval and Renaissance Text Studies).

Florescano, Enrique (1999), *The Myth of Quetzalcoatl* (Baltimore, MD: Johns Hopkins University Press).

Gallarotti, Giulo M. (1995), *The Anatomy of an International Monetary Regime: the Classical Gold Standard 1880–1914* (New York: Oxford University Press).

Gebser, Jean (1984), *Everpresent Origin*, trans. Noel Barstad and Algis Mickunas (Athens, OH: Ohio University Press).

Guthrie, Jill (ed. 1996), *The Olmec World: Ritual and Rulership* (Princeton, NJ: The Art Museum, Princeton University).

Guthrie, W.K.C. (1993), *Orpheus and Greek Religion* (Princeton, NJ: Princeton University Press).

Havelock, Eric (1991), *Preface to Plato* (Cambridge: Cambridge University Press).

Heath, Peter (1992), *Allegory and Philosophy in Avicenna (Ibn Sina) With a Translation of the Book of the Prophet Mohammad's Ascent to Heaven* (Philadelphia, PA: University of Pennsylvania Press).

Higonnet, Patrice (2002), *Paris: Capital of the World* (Cambridge, MA: Harvard University Press).

Hornung, Erik (1999), *The Ancient Egyptian Books of the Afterlife*, trans. David Lorton (Ithaca, NY: Cornell University Press).

Jaynes, Julian (1976), *The Origin of Consciousness in the Breakdown of the Bicameral Mind* (Boston, MA: Houghton Mifflin).

Jones, Charles (ed. 1950), 'The vision of Paul', in *Medieval Literature in Translation* (New York: Longmans, Green).

Jordan, David (1995), *Transforming Paris: The Life and Labors of Baron Haussmann* (Chicago: University of Chicago Press).

Katz, M., Marsh, W., and Thompson, G. (1977), *Earth's Answer: Explorations of Planetary Culture at the Lindisfarne Conferences* (New York: Harper & Row).

Kolinsky, Dorothy and Andel, Jaroslav (ed. 1998), *Frantisek Kupka: Die Abstrakten Farben des Universums* (Verlag Gerd Hatje: Ostfildern bei Stuttgart).

Kramer, Samuel Noah (1963), *The Sumerians: Their History, Culture, and Character* (University of Chicago Press: Chicago and London).

Lakoff, George and Núñez, Raphael (2000), *Where Mathematics Comes From: How the Embodied Mind Brings Mathematics into Being* (New York: Basic Books).

Lévy-Bruhl, Lucien (1925), *La Mentalité Primitive* (Paris: F. Alcan).

Lewis, Bernard (2002), *What Went Wrong? Western Impact and Middle Eastern Response* (New York: Oxford University Press).

Miller, Arthur I. (2001), *Einstein and Picasso: Space, Time, and the Beauty that Creates Havoc* (New York: Basic Books).

Mookerjee, Ajit (1982), *Kundalini: The Arousal of the Inner Energy* (London: Thames and Hudson).

Odyssey (1990), *The Odyssey of Homer*, trans. Robert Fitzgerald (New York: Vintage Classics).

Peterson, Mark A. (1979), 'Dante and the 3-sphere', *American Journal of Physics*, 47 (12), pp. 1031–5.

Redfield, Robert (1953), *The Primitive World and its Transformations* (Ithaca, NY: Cornell University Press).

Shlain, Leonard (1998), *The Alphabet Versus the Goddess* (New York: Viking).

Snell, Bruno (1982), *The Discovery of the Mind in Greek Philosophy and Literature* (New York: Dover Publications).

Stille, Alexander (2002), 'Radical new views about Islam and the Koran', *New York Times*, March 2, 2002, pp. A1–A19.

Teilhard de Chardin, Pierre (1964), *The Future of Man* (New York: Harper & Row).

Thompson, William Irwin (1978), *Darkness and Scattered Light* (New York: Doubleday Anchor Books).

Thompson, William Irwin (1981/1996), *The Time Falling Bodies Take to Light: Mythology, Sexuality, and the Origins of Culture* (New York: St. Martin's Press).

Thompson, William Irwin (1983), *Blue Jade from the Morning Star: a Cycle of Poems and an Essay on Quetzalcoatl* (Hudson, NY: Lindisfarne Press).

Thompson, William Irwin (1985), 'The Four cultural-ecologies of the west' in *Pacific Shift* (San Francsico, CA: Sierra Club Books).

Thompson, William Irwin (1989), 'A cultural history of consciousness' in *Imaginary Landscape: Making Worlds of Myth and Science* (New York: St. Martin's Press).

Thompson, William Irwin (1998), *Coming into Being: Artifacts and Texts in the Evolution of Consciousness* (New York: St. Martin's Press).

Todd, Nancy Jack and Todd, John (1994), *From Eco-Cities to Living Machines: Principles of Ecological Design* (Berkeley, CA: North Atlantic Books).

Turner, Howard R. (1995), *Science in Medieval Islam* (Austin, TX: University of Texas Press).

Werner, Heinz (1957), *The Comparative Psychology of Mental Development* (New York: International Universities Press).

Wolkstein, Diane and Kramer, Samuel Noah (1983), *Inanna, Queen of Heaven and Earth* (New York: Harper Collins).

SOCIETAS: essays in political and cultural criticism

Public debate has been impoverished by two competing trends. On the one hand the trivialization of the media means that in-depth commentary has given way to the ten second soundbite. On the other hand the explosion of knowledge has increased specialization, and academic discourse is no longer comprehensible. As a result writing on politics and culture is either superficial or baffling.

This was not always so — especially for political debate. The high point of the English political pamphlet was the seventeenth century, when a number of small printer-publishers responded to the political ferment of the age with an outpouring of widely-accessible pamphlets and tracts. But in recent years the tradition of the political pamphlet has declined—with most publishers rejecting anything under 100,000 words. The result is that many a good idea ends up drowning in a sea of verbosity. However the introduction of the digital press makes it possible to re-create a more exciting age of publishing. *Societas* authors are all experts in their own field, but the essays are for a general audience. Each book can be read in an evening. The books are available retail at the price of £8.95/$17.90 each, or on bi-monthly subscription for only £5/$10. Details/updated schedule at **imprint-academic.com/societas**

IMPRINT ACADEMIC, PO Box 200, Exeter, EX5 5YX, UK
Tel: (0)1392 841600   Fax: (0)1392 841478   sandra@imprint.co.uk

SOCIETAS

essays in political and cultural criticism

imprint-academic.com/societas

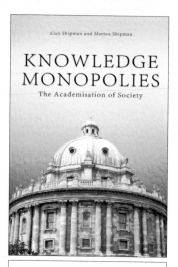

Knowledge Monopolies
Alan Shipman and Marten Shipman

Historians and sociologists chart the *consequences* of the expansion of knowledge; philosophers of science examine the *causes*. This book bridges the gap. The focus is on the paradox whereby, as the general public becomes better educated to live and work with knowledge, the 'academy' increases its intellectual distance, so that the nature of reality becomes more rather than less obscure.

96 pp., £8.95/$17.90

The Referendum Roundabout
Kieron O'Hara

A lively and sharp critique of the role of the referendum in modern British politics. The 1975 vote on Europe is the lens to focus the subject, and the upcoming referendum on the European constitution is also clearly in the author's sights.

Kieron O'Hara is author of *Trust: From Socrates to Spin* (2004) and *After Blair: Conservatism Beyond Thatcher* (2005) and *Plato and the Internet* (2002).

96 pp., £8.95/$17.90

Doing Less With Less
Making Britain More Secure
Paul Robinson

Don't believe neoconservative rhetoric on the 'war on terror': the twenty first century will be much safer. Armed forces designed for the cold war (and only maintained by vested interests within the defence bureaucracy) encourage global interference through pre-emption and other forms of military interventionism. We would be safer with less.

Paul Robinson has served as an army officer and is currently assistant director of the Centre for Security Studies at the University of Hull. His books include *The Just War in Comparative Perspective* (2003).

96 pp., £8.95/$17.90

The Case Against the Democratic State

Gordon Graham

We are now so used to the state's pre-eminence in all things that few think to question it. This essay contends that the gross imbalance of power in the modern state is in need of justification, and that democracy simply masks this need with an illusion of popular sovereignty. Although the arguments are accessible to all, it is written within the European philosophical tradition. The author is Professor of Moral Philosophy at the Uniiversity of Aberdeen. 96 p., £8.95/$17.90

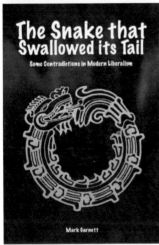

The Snake that Swallowed its Tail

Mark Garnett

Liberal values are the hallmark of a civilised society. Yet they depend on an optimistic view of the human condition, Stripped of this essential ingredient, liberalism has become a hollowed-out abstraction. Tracing its effects through the media, politics and the public services, the author argues that hollowed-out liberalism has helped to produce our present discontent. Unless we stop boasting about our values and try to recover their essence, liberal society will be crushed in the coils of its own contradictions.   96 pp., £8.95/$17.90

The Party's Over

Keith Sutherland

The book argues that the tyranny of the modern political party should be replaced by a mixed constitution in which advocacy is entrusted to an aristocracy of merit, and democratic representation is achieved via a jury-style lottery. 200 pp., £8.95/$17.90

- *'An extremely valuable contribution–a subversive and necessary read.'* **Graham Allen MP**, *Tribune*
- *'His analysis of what is wrong is superb . . . No one can read this book without realising that something radical, even revolutionary must be done.'* **Sir Richard Body**, *Salisbury Review*
- *'A political essay in the best tradition: shrewd, erudite, polemical, partisan, mischievous and highly topical.'* **Contemporary Political Theory**

Darwinian Conservatism
Larry Arnhart

Darwinian biology sustains conservative social thought by showing how the human capacity for spontaneous order arises from social instincts and a moral sense shaped by natural selection in human evolution.

Larry Arnhart is a professor of political science at Northern Illinois University. He is the author of *Aristotle on Political Reasoning*, *Political Questions: Political Philosophy from Plato to Rawls*, and *Darwinian Natural Right: The Biological Ethics of Human Nature*.

96 pp., £8.95/$17.90

The Great Abdication
Alexander Deane

Our middle class has abstained from its responsibility to uphold societal values, and the enormously damaging collapse of our society's norms and standards is largely a result of that abdication. The institutions of political and social governance provide a husk of functionality and mask these problems for those that do not wish to see, or do not care. To restore Britain to something resembling a substantively functioning country, the middle classes must reinstate themselves as arbiters of morality, be unafraid to judge their fellow men, and follow through with the condemnation that necessarily follows when individuals sin against common values.

96 pp., £8.95/$17.90

The Moral Mind
Henry Haslam

Haslam shows how important the moral sense is to the human personality and exposes the weakness in much current thinking that suggests otherwise. His goal is to help the reader to a mature and confident understanding of the moral mind, which constitutes an essential part of what it is to be human. The author writes from from a Judaeo-Christian background and addresses both believers and non-believers.

96 pp., £8.95/$17.90